Routledge Revivals

The Eurodollar Market and the Years of Crisis

First published in 1983, *The Eurodollar Market and the Years of Crisis* embraces the wider concepts of the market's role in international monetary developments and examines the Eurodollar market within the context of the international monetary crisis of 1968- 1974. The book deals primarily with the period leading up to these crises from 1958, during which time the market exerted its greatest impact on the international monetary system. The technical details of the market's structure and functioning are clearly defined, and the second half of the book is devoted to a detailed and systematic chronological investigation of the market's role from its inception in 1958 up to the present times. This is an important historical reference work for students of economics.

The Eurodollar Market and the Years of Crisis

Daniel R. Kane

Routledge Revivals
Routledge
Taylor & Francis Group

First published in 1983
by Croom Helm

This edition first published in 2025 by Routledge
4 Park Square, Milton Park, Abingdon, Oxon, OX14 4RN

and by Routledge
605 Third Avenue, New York, NY 10158

Routledge is an imprint of the Taylor & Francis Group, an informa business

Publisher's Note
The publisher has gone to great lengths to ensure the quality of this reprint but points out that some imperfections in the original copies may be apparent.

Disclaimer
The publisher has made every effort to trace copyright holders and welcomes correspondence from those they have been unable to contact.

A Library of Congress record exists under ISBN: 0709915225

ISBN: 978-1-041-11768-1 (hbk)
ISBN: 978-1-003-66463-5 (ebk)
ISBN: 978-1-041-12415-3 (pbk)

Book DOI 10.4324/9781003664635

The Eurodollar Market and the Years of Crisis

DANIEL R. KANE

St. Martin's Press, Inc., 175 Fifth Avenue, New York, N.Y. 10010
Printed in Great Britain
First published in the United States of America in 1983

Library of Congress Cataloguing in Publication Data

Kane, Daniel R., 1949-
The Eurodollar market and the years of crisis.

1. Eurodollar market. 2. International finance.
I. Title.
HG3897.K35 1983 332.4'5 82-16828
ISBN 0-312-26735-5

CONTENTS

LIST OF FIGURES

LIST OF TABLES

PREFACE

The Euro-dollar market has been the subject of numerous investigations by economists and bankers alike, but these have been largely concentrated either on very general descriptions of the market and its operation or on narrower quantitative analyses of specific aspects of market activity. This polarisation has tended to detract from a clear understanding of the role of the Euro-dollar market both within the wider context of international monetary affairs and, more especially, within the narrower confines of the critical events of the sixties and seventies which helped to shape the international monetary system.

This study is an attempt to identify the role played by the Euro-dollar market and to assess its contribution to developments affecting the international monetary system during these years of crisis.

An expression of sincere thanks must be extended to the many people who have contributed in diverse ways to the preparation of this book, in particular to Mr W. Robertson and Dr F. Meyer for their advice and guidance in the initial stages of the work.

Above all, I wish to thank my wife, Dr June Kane, without whose support and editorial assistance this work would never have been possible. This book is for her.

Chapter One

THE ESTABLISHMENT OF THE MARKET AND ITS FORMATIVE YEARS

THE ESTABLISHMENT OF THE MARKET

It was a diversity of political and economic factors arising in the early and mid-fifties which ultimately led to the establishment of a European market for dollars -- a market which commanded its own interest rate structure, established a further interest rate parity to which forward exchange rates could adjust, financed national payments deficits and possessed the capacity for international exchange reserve augmentation.[1]

Perhaps the earliest political factor of significance was the Soviet fear of seizure or blocking of dollar balances by the US in the event of an outbreak of hostilities. In a desire to avoid such risks, the Soviets transferred their dollar balances to European banks, where they were camouflaged and hence protected. The Moscow Narodny Bank in London and the Banque Commerciale pour l'Europe du Nord in Paris, principal recipients of these funds, attempted to deploy them in a more profitable form than traditional US investments by onlending them as dollar-denominated foreign currency deposits. The demand for these deposits was subsequently augmented by the 1957 sterling support measures which imposed restrictions on third-party sterling trade credits and reduced sterling's role as an international financing medium.

The increasingly widespread use of dollar-denominated foreign currency deposits was similarly fostered by the actions and accommodating attitudes of central monetary authorities. The market was viewed by the Germans as a convenient channel through which dollar reserves could be reduced, by the Italians as an additional source of dollar financing, by the Swiss as a profitable outlet for the deployment of trustee funds and by the British as a means of benefitting the UK balance of payments and enhancing London's role as an international entrepôt centre. The US authorities also encouraged the use of European dollar balances, albeit indirectly, through the inflexible and non-selective use of Regulation Q, which prohibited the payment of interest on demand deposits (deposits with maturities of less than thirty days) and limited the payment of interest on all other time deposits. European banks, in contrast, were free to pay market-determined rates on all dollar deposits, regardless of maturity -- a competitive advantage which extended to the lending side of the market, since European banks were not party to dollar cartel agreements, did not require compensating balances and were not subject to either deposit insurance or statutory reserve requirements on foreign currency liabilities. These advantages of higher returns and greater liquidity, moreover, were not achieved at the expense of greater political or financial risk, since trading tended to be concentrated on politically stable centres such as London and Paris and confined to prime European banks and the overseas branches of prime US banks.

A final factor contributing to the growth of European dollar activity and the establishment of the Euro-dollar market was the stability and confidence provided by the existing order of fixed exchange rates combined with the substantial US net liquidity deficits of the fifties. The former limited exchange rate fluctuations and thus enabled the risks associated with the accepting, placing and arbitraging of deposits to be evaluated and more effectively hedged, whilst the latter placed a substantial $17 billion at the disposal of US non-residents.

The exact point of transformation of this European market for dollars into the Euro-dollar market per se cannot be determined with any certainty. It may be asserted, however, that the process of European dollar activity had become sufficiently well-developed in the late fifties for the Euro-dollar market to have become firmly established by the end of the decade -- a process reflected in the growth of UK banks' external dollar liabilities which effectively doubled from a negligible $157 million in 1957 to $308 million in 1958 to reach $1.6 billion by 1960 (table 1).

THE FORMATIVE YEARS

The Influence of Central Monetary Authorities

The growth of the Euro-dollar market in the early sixties was fostered by the direct and indirect intervention of central monetary authorities in the form of direct dollar depositing, directives requiring that banks adopt or abandon balanced external positions, and commercial bank dollar swaps which also proved the most prevalent form of market intervention.

Dollar swaps were undertaken principally to reduce excess exchange reserves and to regulate domestic liquidity levels. They served to divert to the market deposits which might otherwise have remained in "pure" deposit form in the US and were conducted with varying degrees of intensity throughout this period. Prominent amongst authorities undertaking swap transactions was the Bundesbank, which engaged in frequent and extensive swaps following the establishment of convertibility in 1958. The German economy had been characterised in the fifties by an almost uninterrupted surplus on current account which, for the decade as a whole, had amounted to DM 34.6 billion, with the individual years of 1957 and 1958 accounting for surpluses of DM 5.9 billion and DM 6.0 billion respectively. In an attempt to reduce the resultant exchange reserves, the Bundesbank engaged in extensive swap transactions with domestic commercial banks. Initially these swaps were offered at a "flat" rate (at equal spot and forward rates), but this proved insufficiently attractive and consequently in 1960 the Bundesbank began to subsidise its swap facilities by offering dollars at a forward premium which rose to a maximum 1½% p.a. by September of that year. A subsequent decline in domestic interest rates and the emergence of a current account deficit, however, led to the removal of the premium in March 1962 and the eventual unwinding of swap commitments by March 1963. At their peak in early 1962, outstanding swaps amounted to just over $1 billion. The subsequent re-emergence of a current account surplus in the fourth quarter of 1963, however, and a sustained long-term capital inflow for the year as a whole, prompted the Bundesbank to resume swap operations in March 1964 although on this occasion swaps were restricted to periods of three months or longer and had to be used specifically for the purchase of US money market instruments, basically in recognition of the fact that dollars deposited in the Euro-dollar market were likely to be recycled to the Bundesbank, thereby exacerbating exchange rate pressures and inflating official dollar reserves.

Intervention in the market by the Italian authorities assumed all three forms: swaps, direct deposits and the regulation of domestic banks' net foreign currency positions. Italian banks had been active borrowers of European dollar deposits from the early fifties, but it was not until after convertibility that borrowings began to assume significant proportions and it was partly in response to the magnitude of these borrowings and the high domestic liquidity engendered that the Bank of Italy sought to reduce banks' lira reserves by offering dollar swaps and instructing banks to balance their foreign currency positions. The low liquidity of the early 1960s, in contrast, subjected banks' reserve ratios to increasing pressure which the Bank of Italy alleviated by converting outstanding dollar swaps into direct dollar deposits such that, at their peak in 1962, central monetary claims on domestic commercial banks amounted to $1 billion. In November 1962, following a reduction in the Italian balance of payments surplus, banks were exempted from the need to maintain balanced external positions and proceeded to establish themselves, once again, as net borrowers in the Euro-dollar market.

In addition to German and Italian intervention in the market, other monetary authorities either tacitly approved of, actively encouraged or directly utilised the Euro-dollar market and its facilities. The UK authorities tacitly condoned UK involvement in the market (official approval of entrepôt trading already existed) by sanctioning Local Authority "Euro-dollar borrowing" in the form of Euro-dollar deposits swapped into sterling for the purpose of extending loans to Local Authorities. The Swiss National Bank, less covertly, deposited with Swiss commercial banks dollars received in the form of Federal Reserve swaps, while the Belgian authorities not only resorted to Euro-dollars to accommodate part of their budget deficits, but also financed sales of Treasury bills to commercial banks with domestic currency swaps. Even the Soviet authorities, acting through the Moscow Narodny Bank, intervened to secure official dollar financing in the market.

Official intervention in the form of deposits, swaps and regulatory measures to exploit the Euro-dollar market and its facilities thus not only amounted to the explicit condoning of the market's existence but also contributed directly to both the growth and development of Euro-dollar activity.

Interest Rate Constraints

The major determinant of market activity in the early sixties was not the availability of Euro-dollar credits (significant as this became in the late sixties), but the relatively low cost of credits in comparison to their US and European counterparts which were subject to both private and official interest rate constraints.

The most important constraints were undoubtedly those operating in the US, since it was the relatively low deposit ceilings imposed by Regulation Q and the relatively high lending floor determined by the US prime rate which provided the trading margins within which the Euro-dollar market could operate. The low deposit ceilings were a consequence of Regulation Q, which was not only a blunt and unsophisticated means of depressing domestic interest rates, but had also been applied inflexibly since its inception in 1933 (in the period 1957 to 1963, for example, interest rates on deposits with maturities of 90 - 179 days had been subject to a ceiling of 2½% p.a.). These ceilings provided overseas banks with considerable scope to pay higher rates than those payable not only on US deposits but also, as may be seen from figure 1-1 (p.6) on US bankers' acceptances and US Treasury bills. The relatively high lending rate floor, in contrast, was determined by institutional and administrative as well as market factors. Between August 1960 and December 1965 the US prime rate remained unchanged at 4½% and it was this inability to respond to changing market conditions which enabled Euro-banks to effectively compete with credits of US origin. The competitive advantage

Figure 1-1

US BANKS' PRIME RATES, REGULATION Q THREE-MONTH DEPOSIT RATE MAXIMA AND INTEREST RATES ON SELECTED THREE-MONTH US MONEY MARKET INSTRUMENTS[1] AND THREE-MONTH EURO-DOLLAR DEPOSITS[2]
1960 - 1963

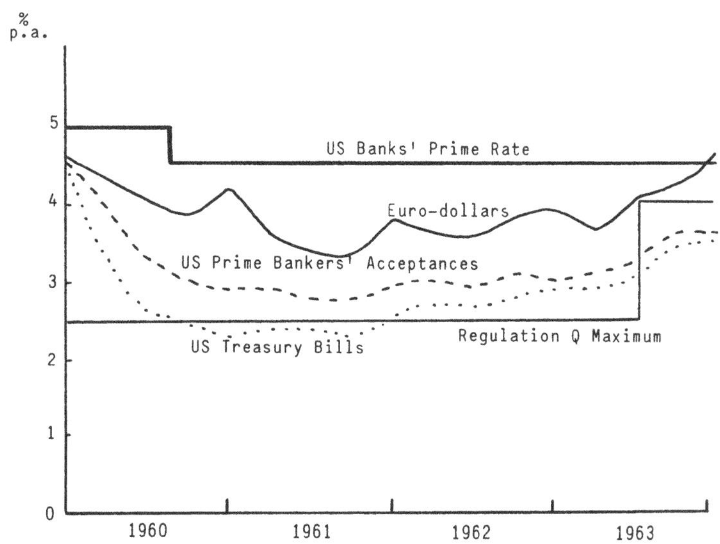

1. Average of last month of quarter
2. End of quarter

Sources: Federal Reserve Bulletin, various issues
Bank of England Quarterly Bulletin, various issues

of Euro-banks was also enhanced by the US practice of requiring borrowers to maintain compensating balances of 10% to 20% of loans in time or, more frequently, demand deposit accounts. The exact size of these balances varied with the standing of the customer and, to a lesser extent, the state of the market but the net effect was to raise the real cost of borrowing above the nominal rate. The effective prime rate for the period 1960 to 1965 was thus not 4½% but a figure more closely approaching 5% - 5½%.[2] Even this practice of maintaining compensating balances understated the true impact of interest rate constraints, however, for only a minority of borrowers were accorded prime status in US markets and foreign borrowers who might generally have expected to secure credits at the keenest (prime) rates in their respective domestic markets were frequently charged between ¼% and ½% over prime rate to compensate for the extra "risk" involved. Moreover, even those borrowers who might have been able to secure credits at prime rates often resorted to Euro-dollars to avoid compliance with the detailed US financial disclosures required of foreign borrowers. The result of these ceilings and floors, therefore, was to raise the effective spread between US banks' deposit and loan rates from the 2% of figure 1-1 to a figure more closely approaching 3% - 5½%, and it was by operating within this spread that the Euro-dollar market was able to mount and sustain its effective challenge to the US market.

Interest rate constraints did not only operate in the US, for many European countries sanctioned and enforced similar cartel restrictions. Lira loans to prime commercial borrowers, for example, were extended in accordance with a minimum scale of rates determined by a "gentleman's agreement" amongst Italian commercial banks. In 1960 an attempt was made to extend this agreement to loans denominated in foreign currencies, but the rigour of Euro-dollar competition ensured that this attempt remained largely ineffective. Similar agreements and impediments to domestic currency competition operated in countries such as France, Switzerland, Germany, Holland and the UK, with the result that foreign currency loans could frequently be secured more cheaply than comparable domestic credits.

Interest rates thus proved an important

determinant of Euro-dollar activity in the early sixties, when access to New York's capital markets was still relatively easy and emphasis had not yet shifted away from the cost to the availability of Euro-dollar credits.

US Balance of Payments Restraints

The US Interest Equalization Tax (IET), by denying foreign borrowers free access to long-term US capital markets, ushered in the transition from cost to availability as the prime determinant of Euro-dollar competitiveness. The tax was enacted in September 1964 retroactively operational from July 1963 and was designed to reduce long-term capital outflows without increasing domestic interest rates. It was levied on US purchases of foreign securities and ranged from a flat 15% for stocks to a maximum 15% for bonds with outstanding maturities of more than 28 years. The competitiveness of US security markets was such, however, that the cost of the tax, which amounted to an average one percentage point per annum on foreign bonds issued in the US, was effectively borne by foreign borrowers who responded by curtailing their US financing demand and transfering part of this demand to the Euro-dollar market. The effect of this displacement and indirectly, therefore, the effect on the Euro-dollar market was most clearly manifested in the reduction of new foreign issues in the US which declined from $1.6 billion in the twelve months ending June 1963 to $672 million in the twelve months to June 1964.

The process of disfranchising US capital markets from foreign borrowers was reinforced by the 1965 Voluntary Foreign Credit Restraint Program (VFCRP) -- and, later, by the 1968 Foreign Direct Investment Program (FDIP)[3] -- which was designed to improve the US balance of payments by imposing further constraints on US capital outflows. The major provisions of the programme were:

-- IET was extended to include bank credits with maturities of twelve months or more and US purchases of foreign bonds with remaining maturities of 1 - 3 years (both of which had been excluded from the 1964 provisions of the tax);

-- US banks were requested to restrict the growth of their lending to foreigners in

1965 to 105% of the level outstanding at the end of 1964;

-- US non-bank financial institutions were requested not only to refrain from increasing their liquid claims on foreigners but also to reduce the level of such claims in 1965 to the levels outstanding at the end of 1963. They were also requested to refrain from accommodating financing demands previously refused by banks;

-- Non-banks (essentially corporations) were required to improve their individual balance of payments with developed countries by 15% - 20% either on trade account or through increased borrowing, and to reduce the level of short-term assets held in these countries.

The effect of these restrictions was to accentuate the market distortions and institutional rigidities previously introduced by the Interest Equalization Tax and to subject the Euro-dollar market to both expansionary and, to a lesser extent, contractionary forces. The expansionary impact of the programme was confined to the demand side of the market since the programme's restrictions not only obliged US non-residents to channel their financing requirements to European markets but also encouraged US corporations to resort to overseas borrowing for both investment and balance of payments purposes. The programme's contractionary supply impact, in contrast, resulted from the restrictions imposed on US banks' foreign lending, since these served to reduce the supply of deposits potentially flowing to the Euro-dollar market, and from the requirement that non-banks and non-bank financial institutions reduce their outstanding claims on US non-residents, since this threatened to reduce the supply of deposits already existing in the market.

The short-term impact of these influences was to subject the Euro-dollar market to a further round of growth and administratively induced trading activity. On a longer-term basis, IET and the VFCRP contributed to the development of medium-term Euro-dollar credit facilities which, together with the extended terms which banks were prepared to pay to secure deposits, helped to transform the Euro-dollar market from what had hitherto been an essentially short-term money market into a medium-term international capital market.

Consortium Banking

The growing demand for Euro-dollar credits of larger size and longer maturity subjected banks to increasing pressure in the mid-sixties. It was partly in response to this pressure, as well as to the more profitable opportunities afforded by such demands, that the practice of consortium banking evolved. Consortium banks are independent banks collectively owned by shareholding banks, established in order to complement rather than compete with their parent shareholders whilst still exploiting the trading opportunities afforded by this type of structural organisation:

(i) By drawing on both parental and conventional deposit resources, consortium banks were able to extend credits which would otherwise have proved beyond the capacity of individual shareholder banks or else which might have resulted in the over-extending of individual positions;

(ii) By combining both the financial and physical resources of shareholder banks, consortium banks were able to extend credits with long maturities at relatively low costs. The long maturities resulted from consortium banks' being assured of a continuing and stable supply of funds from parent shareholders whilst the relatively low costs were a direct result of banks' ability to dispense with the necessity of maintaining branch outlets to cultivate adequate deposit bases;

(iii) By concentrating on selected areas of banking activity, such as the provision of medium-term Euro-dollar facilities, consortium banks were able to exploit the benefits of specialisation;

(iv) Consortium banking benefitted from "synergetic dynamism", a concept which attracted considerable financial interest in the sixties. Essentially embracing the concept of "the total value of a composite being greater than the sum of the individual values of its component parts", it combined such factors as deposit availability, technical expertise and cost-effectiveness to provide a coherent whole which could trade more profitably than its constituent parts.

Just as London had established itself as the dominant trading centre from the inception of the Euro-dollar market, so it was the first to seize the initiative with respect to consortium banking. The first consortium bank to be established was Midland and International Banks Limited (MAIBL) in 1964, whose shareholders were The Standard Bank (19%), The Toronto Dominion Bank (26%), The Commercial Bank of Australia (10%) and The Midland Bank (45%). It was originally intended that MAIBL should concentrate on medium-term sterling credits, but the sterling problems of the mid-sixties and the subsequent restrictions imposed on sterling-denominated credits occasioned a switch to Euro-dollar lending in much the same way as the sterling restrictions of 1957 had been an important factor contributing to the establishment of the Euro-dollar market in the late fifties. MAIBL rapidly established itself as an important force in Euro-dollar trading and its success spawned a proliferation of competing institutions whose collective impact was significant not only because these banks were innovators within the field of medium-term lending, but also because they contributed to the integration of national and international capital markets through the provision of financing facilities which traditional capital markets had found increasingly difficult to provide.

Negotiable Euro-dollar Certificates of Deposit

A further manifestation of the sophisticated financing machinery developed to cope with the growing demand for Euro-dollar financing was the issuing of negotiable dollar certificates of deposit (CDs) in London in May 1966.[4] The significance of this development lay not just in the rapid growth of new issues, important as this was, --by the June 1974 crisis of confidence the value of outstanding CDs issued in London amounted to $13.8 billion, accounted for almost 10% of total UK Euro-currency positions and involved an estimated monthly turnover approaching $2 billion -- but in the underlying changes in market structure manifested in this growth.

The advent of CDs was indicative of the increasing depth and flexibility demanded of the Euro-dollar market and of the developing awareness and sophistication of market users. The certificates enabled corporate and private operators to adjust their liquidity positions more finely than conventional non-negotiable deposits, whilst simultaneously affording banks greater liquidity through the trading of CDs on both the issuing and accepting sides of the market. These benefits served to strengthen the market's structure and enhance the flexibility of its deposit facilities.

London CDs also proved significant as an acceptable investment substitute for US CDs whose controlled rates formed part of the authorities' attempts to regulate economic activity through monetary targets and interest rate ceilings. The outflow of US funds subsequent to the operation of these ceilings was directed towards London CDs and proved an important stimulus to the growth of market activity in 1966 and to the attendant development of US banks' Euro-dollar borrowing.

US Banks' Euro-dollar Borrowing

The emergence of a sustained and substantial volume of Euro-dollar borrowing by US banks in 1966 was important both in its own right and because it established the pattern of events which were to contribute to the destabilising flows of 1969.

The predominant stimulus to this borrowing was the 1966 US monetary restraint programme which was initiated in December 1965 when the discount rate was raised from 4% to 4½% and the prime rate raised -- for the first time in over five years -- from 4½% to 5%. These measures were subsequently reinforced in 1966 by the raising of reserve requirements on time deposits from 4% to 6% and the lowering of Regulation Q ceilings on multiple-maturity time deposits from 5½% to 4% and from 5½% to 5% for deposits with maturities of less and more than 90 days respectively.

The effect of these measures was to raise interest rates on secondary market CDs to levels above Q ceilings and to create interest differentials on new issues of CDs amounting to 100 basis points in favour of Euro-dollars. This generated substantial reserve losses and a rapid attrition of CDs, which declined by a substantial $2.7 billion in the six weeks ending October 1966. It was in an attempt to finance these reserve losses and redress the attrition of CDs that US banks turned to Euro-dollar borrowing.

US banks' Euro-dollar borrowing principally assumed the form of increases in liabilities to overseas branches and such was the magnitude of this borrowing that liabilities to overseas branches increased from an end-of-month average of $1.5 billion in 1965 to $2 billion by mid-1966 and thereafter accelerated rapidly to reach $4 billion by the end of the year. Whilst not all of this borrowing originated in Europe, the overwhelming majority was accounted for by Euro-dollar flows, a fact which was reflected in the almost threefold increase in head office claims reported by the UK branches of US banks. These claims increased from $975 million at the end of 1965 to $2.8 billion by the end of 1966 and corresponded to an increase in the US's net absorption of Euro-dollars from $1.3 billion in 1965 to $3.3 billion in 1966 (table 2). Accompanying these flows was a marked reaction in three-month Euro-dollar rates which increased from an already high base of 5.2% in November 1965 to an historic peak of 7.2% by November 1966 (table 3).

The emergence of US banks' Euro-dollar borrowing thus exerted a discrete and powerful short-term impact on the Euro-dollar market. It was the longer-term repercussions, however, which served to differentiate this borrowing from a simple increase in Euro-dollar activity:

Firstly, the borrowing represented a transition from US banks' previous practice of "passively" borrowing deposits -- as arose, for example, when overseas branches placed deposits surplus to immediate requirements with their US head offices -- to one of "active" borrowing, whereby foreign branches directly solicited deposits to finance US banks' domestic operations. The implications of this transition subsequently proved of critical importance to both the development of the Euro-dollar market and the operation of US and, increasingly, European monetary policies.

Secondly, with negative US/Euro-dollar interest rate differentials, the borrowing served to further dispel the notion that the Euro-dollar market could only operate within the interest rate constraints determined by US money markets.

Thirdly, and perhaps most significantly, the impact of US banks' borrowing on the Euro-dollar market proved considerably more durable than the actual borrowings themselves, since the emergence of this borrowing served to introduce into the market a permanent element of demand which was determined essentially by US economic conditions. The effect of this was to forge a powerful link between US, Euro-dollar and European markets and to further expose European capital markets to the vicissitudes of US domestic monetary policy.

1966 marked a turning point for the Euro-dollar market. It was a year in which the emergence of sustained and substantial US banks' Euro-dollar borrowing, which established the pattern for the destabilising flows of the late sixties and early seventies, signalled the end of the market's formative years and the beginning of a period in which the market would not only play an increasingly active international financing role but would eventually contribute both directly and indirectly to the crises which ultimately led to the restructuring of the entire international monetary system.

The years of crisis were indeed at hand.

NOTES

1. For a comprehensive definition of Euro-dollars and the problems of market quantification, see Appendix A, pp.127-131.

2. The real cost of borrowing is:

$$\text{Real Rate} = \frac{\text{Nominal Rate}}{1 - \text{Compensating Balance Rate}}$$

With a prime rate of 4½% and compensating balances of 20%, the real rate is 5.6%.

3. The 1968 Foreign Direct Investment Program (FDIP) supplemented the 1965 VFCRP with mandatory controls on selected capital flows in an attempt to limit reserve losses and curb capital outflows. The major provisions of the programme as they related to the Euro-dollar market were:

<u>Banks</u>

-- a reduction in the ceiling on banks' foreign loans to 103% of the base figure outstanding at the end of 1964;

-- a reduction of 40%, during 1968, in the level of short-term credits outstanding to continental Western European countries at the end of December 1967;

-- a requirement that banks should refrain from renewing existing, or from offering new term loans to continental Western Europe.

Non-bank Financial Institutions

-- a reduction in foreign assets in 1968 to 95% of the totals outstanding at the end of 1967;

-- with the exception of minimum working balances, a reduction to zero in liquid claims held abroad.

Non-banking concerns

-- a moratorium on direct investment outflows to continental Western Europe (this, significantly, excluded investment financed out of overseas borrowings);

-- direct investors to remit a percentage of earnings equal to the average remitted in the years 1964-1966;

-- by June 1968, short-term foreign claims to be reduced to the average end-of-month levels prevailing in 1965 and 1966.

4. Negotiable dollar certificates of deposit are negotiable receipts for dollars which have been deposited with banks for periods ranging typically from one month to five years. The certificates may be issued on tap or tranche basis, generally for minimum sums of $25,000.

Chapter Two

THE 1968 GOLD CRISIS

THE ONSET OF THE CRISIS

The March 1968 gold crisis was the first to occur in which the Euro-dollar market was capable of playing a direct financing role. It thus affords the twofold opportunity of examining the role of the market in an event which signified a radical departure from the rigid monetary framework of Bretton Woods and of beginning to construct a profile of the Euro-dollar market as a speculative financing vehicle.

The final quarter of 1967 was characterised by heavy demand for gold, prompted essentially by concern over the earlier devaluation of sterling, the deteriorating US balance of payments and the continuing stability of the dollar. Despite official attempts to assuage doubts about the dollar's immutability and to restore confidence in the currency's gold link, renewed buying pressure developed in early March 1968 and continued to intensify until Friday March 15th, when the London gold market was closed and a two-tier gold market was established under the terms of the Washington Agreement.

The two principal characteristics of the gold crisis were the intensity of demand and the relatively short period in which this was manifested. Estimates of gold demand may be derived from production, uses and sales data which indicate that, in the first quarter of 1968, \$360 million of new gold production together with a \$1410 million decline in world monetary gold stocks accommodated a \$1770 million increase in private gold absorption, \$210 million being accounted for by artistic and industrial uses, leaving \$1560 million to be accounted for by speculative/

precautionary purchases (figure 2-1, p. 18). The financing of this sum clearly involved a major international financing operation which may be examined to determine to what extent, if at all, the Euro-dollar market may have contributed to such financing.

EURO-DOLLAR FINANCING POSSIBILITIES

Withdrawal of Deposits

The first possibility concerns the withdrawal of Euro-dollar deposits by private claimants to finance gold purchases. If non-official depositors withdraw funds from the Euro-dollar market to finance the purchase of gold from official institutions, which in turn finance the acquisition of gold from the US by drawing on US held dollar reserves, the net result will be a decline in world gold reserves and a decline in US liabilities to non-official foreigners, since the original decline in official dollar holdings will have been offset by a transfer of dollars from private to official claimants. There will also be a decline in Euro-dollar assets and liabilities corresponding to the dollars withdrawn to finance the private gold purchases.

Secondly, if central monetary institutions hold their dollar reserves in the form of Euro-dollars (identified official holdings of Euro-dollars amounted to $2.2 billion at the end of 1967 -- table 4), and subsequently redeposit their sale receipts in the Euro-dollar market, there will be no impact on US liabilities to official foreigners since the latters' claims will be recorded as a residual in international payments data. Thus a withdrawal of private Euro-dollars to finance gold purchases will result in a net decline in international gold reserves, a decline in US liabilities to non-official foreigners corresponding to an equal decline in Euro-dollar assets and liabilities, and no change in official dollar reserves held as Euro-dollar deposits and recorded in international payments data as a reserve residual.

Neither of these financing possibilities accords with the flow patterns observed in the first quarter of 1968, however, since an expansion, rather than a contraction in Euro-dollar liabilities

Figure 2-1

PRINCIPAL NET GOLD FLOWS
December 1967 - March 1968

($ millions)

Decline in world monetary gold stocks	1410
Increase in production	360
Total supply forthcoming	1770
Estimated industrial and artistic use	210
Estimated speculative/precautionary purchases	1560

Source: IMF Annual Report, 1968

Figure 2-2

EURO-DOLLAR INTEREST RATES AND GOLD PRICES
March 8th - 22nd 1968

	London Gold Price ($/ounce)	Paris Gold Price ($/ounce)	Euro-dollar Bid and Offer Rates (% pa) Call	7-day	3-month
Fri 8th	$35.19\frac{3}{4}$	--	$5\frac{1}{8} - 5\frac{5}{8}$	$5\frac{1}{4} - 5\frac{3}{4}$	$5\frac{5}{8} - 6\frac{1}{8}$
Mon 11th	$35.19\frac{7}{8}$	--	$5\frac{1}{4} - 5\frac{3}{4}$	$5\frac{3}{8} - 5\frac{7}{8}$	$5\frac{5}{8} - 6\frac{1}{8}$
Tue 12th	$35.19\frac{5}{8}$	--	$5\frac{1}{8} - 5\frac{5}{8}$	$5\frac{3}{4} - 6\frac{1}{4}$	$5\frac{7}{8} - 6\frac{3}{8}$
Wed 13th	$35.19\frac{3}{4}$	--	$5\frac{1}{4} - 5\frac{3}{4}$	$5\frac{1}{2} - 6$	$6 - 6\frac{1}{2}$
Thu 14th	$35.19\frac{7}{8}$	--	$5\frac{1}{2} - 6$	$5\frac{1}{2} - 6$	$6\frac{5}{8} - 7\frac{3}{8}$
Fri 15th	Market Closed	44	$5\frac{1}{2} - 6$	$5\frac{1}{2} - 6$	$6\frac{5}{8} - 7\frac{3}{8}$
Mon 18th	''	40	$5\frac{7}{8} - 6\frac{3}{8}$	$5\frac{7}{8} - 6\frac{3}{8}$	$6\frac{3}{4} - 7\frac{1}{4}$
Tue 19th	''	38	$5\frac{7}{8} - 6\frac{3}{8}$	$6\frac{1}{2} - 7$	$6\frac{5}{8} - 7\frac{1}{8}$
Wed 20th	''	37	$6 - 6\frac{1}{2}$	$6\frac{3}{8} - 6\frac{7}{8}$	$6\frac{3}{8} - 6\frac{7}{8}$
Thu 21st	''	38	$6\frac{1}{8} - 6\frac{5}{8}$	$6\frac{3}{8} - 6\frac{7}{8}$	$6\frac{3}{8} - 6\frac{7}{8}$
Fri 22nd	''	39	$6\frac{1}{8} - 6\frac{5}{8}$	$6\frac{3}{8} - 6\frac{7}{8}$	$6\frac{3}{8} - 6\frac{7}{8}$

Source: Financial Times, various issues

was recorded in the first quarter of the year.

A third situation emerges if Euro-dollars are used to finance private gold purchases but the receipts from the sale of monetary gold acquired from the US with official dollars held in the US are redeposited in the Euro-dollar market. If non-US non-official claimants withdraw Euro-dollars to finance the purchase of gold from official institutions which in turn finance the acquisition of gold from the US by drawing on US held dollar reserves, and if the dollars received from private individuals in exchange for gold are subsequently redeposited in the Euro-dollar market, the result will be a net decline in international gold stocks, a decline in US liabilities to foreign officials corresponding to an increase in the international reserve residual, but no change in either US liabilities to non-official foreigners or aggregate Euro-dollar assets or liabilities, since the private financing of gold with Euro-dollars will have merely entailed a redistribution of deposit liabilities away from private to official claimants.

A fourth corresponding financing possibility involves the private purchase of gold with dollars held in the US and the subsequent depositing of official receipts in the Euro-dollar market. Whilst this possibility does not involve a direct withdrawal of Euro-dollar deposits, it demonstrates what may be termed the market's "passive" financing capacity, and may appropriately be incorporated into the present analysis. If non-US non-official claimants withdraw US held dollars to finance the purchase of gold from official institutions which in turn finance the acquisition of gold from the US by drawing on US held dollar reserves, and if the dollars received from private individuals in exchange for gold are subsequently deposited in the Euro-dollar market, the result will be a net decline in international gold stocks, a decline in US liabilities to foreign officials corresponding to an increase in the international reserve residual, and a net increase in Euro-dollar assets and liabilities resulting from the placement of official funds in the market. The contra entry to the increase in Euro-dollar assets (claims on the US) will be an increase in US liabilities to non-official foreigners, but since such liabilities would have already declined as a result of the private purchasing of gold with dollars, there will be no net change in US liabilities to foreign non-officials, but merely a redistribution amongst claimants.

Whilst each of these possibilities is constrained by the growth of the exchange reserve residual, it is readily apparent that possibility three is consistent with a zero change in aggregate market positions and a redistribution of deposit liabilities amongst individual Euro-dollar claimants whilst possibility four is consistent with both a redistribution of US liabilities and a net increase in market positions resulting from the net transfer of official funds from the US to the Euro-dollar market. It thus follows that financing possibilities three and four are the most feasible of the four financing possibilities, since they accord most closely with the flow patterns observed in the first quarter of 1968 and are consistent with the $1.6 billion increase in identified official Euro-dollar holdings recorded that year (table 4). Their practicability, however, is constrained by the $0.4 billion growth in the first quarter's international exchange reserve residual.

Increase in Claims

The use of Euro-dollar claims to finance gold purchases presents three financing possibilities:

Firstly, if Euro-dollars are borrowed to finance gold purchases from official institutions which acquire the gold from the US by drawing on their dollar reserves, and if these institutions subsequently redeposit their dollar receipts in the US, the result will be a decline in monetary gold stocks and US liabilities to foreign non-officials but no change in Euro-dollar assets and liabilities other than the conversion of a Euro-dollar claim on the US into a claim on a private gold purchaser.

Secondly, if Euro-dollars are again borrowed to finance gold purchases from official institutions which acquire the gold from the US by drawing on US held dollar reserves, but on this occasion the dollar receipts are subsequently redeposited in the Euro-dollar market, there will be a decline in monetary gold stocks and US liabilities to foreign officials, but a zero change in US liabilities to foreign non-officials. This change will correspond, moreover, to both an increase in the international exchange reserve residual and a net expansion in Euro-dollar assets and liabilities, since the transfer of official dollar claims to the Euro-dollar market will occasion a net increase in deposit liabilities. If the process were then repeated with Euro-dollars financing second and subsequent rounds of gold purchases, there would be further declines in monetary gold reserves and US liabilities to foreign officials and corresponding increases in aggregate Euro-dollar positions and the international exchange reserve residual.

Thirdly, if Euro-dollars are borrowed to effect gold purchases from official institutions which, on this occasion, acquire the gold from the US by drawing on their Euro-dollar reserves, and if the receipts from the gold sales are subsequently redeposited in the Euro-dollar market,[1] the result will be a decline in monetary gold stocks and US liabilities to non-official foreigners, an expansion in Euro-dollar assets and liabilities but no change in the international exchange reserve residual, since the redepositing of official funds will merely have served to offset the original withdrawal of funds to finance the initial purchase of gold from the US.[2]

The borrowing of Euro-dollars to effect private gold purchases thus generates three financing possibilities which may be summarised as: a decline in US liabilities to foreign non-officials with no change in liabilities to foreign officials; a decline in US liabilities to foreign officials with no change in liabilities to foreign non-officials but a rise in the exchange reserve residual; and finally a decline in US liabilities to foreign non-officials and no change in liabilities to foreign officials, (the decline in monetary gold stocks is common to all).

A comparison of each of these possibilities with the financing flows observed in the first quarter of 1968 reveals that only the second possibility accords with observed flow data. This, together with the two liability financing possibilities which similarly accorded with observed flow data (the purchase of gold with official dollar reserves and the official depositing in the Euro-dollar market of gold sale receipts held originally either in the US or in the Euro-dollar market) would indicate that the Euro-dollar market's ability to finance private speculative/precautionary gold purchases was limited both by the institutional mechanics of the market and by the relatively modest expansion in the exchange reserve residual -- a conclusion endorsed by the following corroboratory data on Euro-dollar flow patterns and interest rate changes.

Corroboratory Data

Changes in Euro-dollar interest rates for the period March 8th to March 22nd 1968, (illustrated in figure 2-2, p. 18), show that changes in Euro-dollar rates in the period leading up to the closure of the London gold market were relatively constrained, with call, seven-day and three-month offer rates increasing by 38, 25 and 125 basis points respectively in the five working days ending Thursday March 14th. These changes suggest that the limited financing demand which did emerge was concentrated at the "longer" end of the market (where spreads between call and three-month offer rates widened from 50 to 138 basis points between Friday March 8th and Thursday March 14th) but that the increases in interest rates were in any case not particularly significant, either absolutely or in relation to the rises recorded in subsequent periods of currency instability.

A second, albeit discrete measure of the Euro-dollar market's financing role involves changes in reporting banks' external dollar positions, (illustrated in figure 2-3, p. 23), which show that aggregate Euro-dollar assets and liabilities increased by $2.4 billion and $2.2 billion respectively in the first quarter of 1968. Whilst this increase in Euro-dollar liabilities would preclude the existence of wholesale deposit withdrawals to finance speculative gold purchases, it does not necessarily follow that increases in Euro-dollar claims were not used for such purposes. It is therefore necessary to distinguish between positions inclusive and exclusive of the US, since such differentiation reveals that a substantial $1.2 billion (50%) of the reported increase in Euro-dollar assets was accounted for by increased claims on the US. Since the greater part of this increase reflected FDIP influences and US banks' Euro-dollar borrowing (US banks' liabilities to their overseas branches increased by $680 million in the first three months of 1968 -- table 5) and since US residents were legally prohibited from purchasing gold, it follows that virtually all this $1.2 billion increase was accounted

Figure 2-3

EXTERNAL DOLLAR POSITIONS OF REPORTING EUROPEAN BANKS
December 1967 - March 1968

($ billions)

		December 1967	March 1968	Ch
	Liabilities	15.6	17.3	-
EXCLUDING US	Assets	13.6	14.8	+
	Net	-2.0	-2.5	-
	Liabilities	2.5	3.0	-
VIS-A-VIS US	Assets	6.3	7.5	+
	Net	+3.8	+4.5	+
	Liabilities	18.1	20.3	-
TIONS	Assets	19.9	22.3	+
	Net	+1.8	+2.0	+

S Annual Report, 1969

for by non-gold uses. Moreover, since the increase in Euro-dollar claims excluding the US was not unrepresentative of increases in immediately preceding and succeeding quarters and since there was no accompanying untoward increase in Euro-dollar rates, this would suggest that the greater part of this increase was similarly used for non-gold financing purposes.

The third and final measure of the market's financing role involves the dollar positions of US banks' foreign branches, US banks' UK branches and UK banks. These positions are of consequence not only because they are well documented, but also because they reflect the dominant role of these banks in Euro-dollar activities.

The dollar liabilities of US banks' foreign branches increased by $567 million in March 1968, of which positions vis-à-vis other foreign branches, official institutions and other foreign banks increased by $105 million, $174 million and $486 million respectively, whilst positions vis-à-vis US residents and other private foreigners declined by $134 million and $63 million respectively. Of these changes the two most important were those reported vis-à-vis official and private claimants: the former because it represented the largest recorded increase since data were first compiled in mid-1966 and therefore suggests the depositing of official gold sale proceeds in the Euro-dollar market, the latter because of the modest size of the withdrawals potentially used for gold financing purposes. Increases in branches' total dollar assets amounted to $730 million, of which the most important component was the $144 million increase in claims on non-bank foreigners, the modest size of this increase again suggesting the limited potential use of Euro-dollars for gold financing purposes.

Reported changes in the dollar positions of US banks'UK branches confirm the broad magnitudes and conclusions derived from total US branches' overseas positions. Of the $642 million increase in aggregate dollar liabilities, the most significant changes were those reported vis-à-vis official institutions and private foreigners, which increased and decreased by $168 million and $108 million respectively. Similarly, of the $236 million increase in total claims, increases on non-bank foreigners accounted for $139 million -- a figure comparable to changes recorded in immediately preceding and succeeding periods.

Changes in UK banks' external dollar positions are an important final indicator of the Euro-dollar market's potential financing role, since they are available on a geographically disaggregated basis and reflect UK banks' dominant role in Euro-dollar activities. In the first quarter of 1968, external dollar liabilities increased by $1 billion distributed equally, on a proportional basis, amongst existing Euro-dollar claimants, indicating that there was no wholesale collective or individual withdrawal of Euro-dollar deposits to finance speculative gold purchases (even liabilities vis-à-vis the Middle East, a traditional gold-hoarding area, recorded a modest increase). Changes in claims proved even more significant for, of the $1.4 billion increase in total claims, $1.1 billion was accounted for by the US, leaving just $300 million to be accounted for by other positions, of which Japan (whose demand for dollars for domestic purposes was substantial) absorbed $130 million. This would again confirm the absence of any significant expansion in Euro-dollar borrowing for speculative gold financing purposes.

A synthesis of the corroboratory data on interest rates and flow patterns reveals that whilst the firming of Euro-dollar rates and the redistribution of Euro-dollar liabilities from private to official claimants indicate the emergence of demand financing pressures and a withdrawal of Euro-dollar deposits, the evidence does not support the wholesale recourse to Euro-dollars as a means of financing the $1.6 billion of private gold purchases recorded in the first quarter of 1968. It may be concluded, therefore, that the Euro-dollar market did not constitute a significant force in the financing of the 1968 gold crisis.

NOTES

1. There is no reason to suppose that in this situation official deposits originally held in the Euro-dollar market will be redeposited in the US subsequent to official gold sales.

2. The expansion in Euro-dollar positions presupposes that the increased demand for Euro-dollar credits would, through higher interest rates, have generated its own supply of credits.

Chapter Three

US BANKS' EURO-DOLLAR BORROWING

The policies which proved so disruptive to both the Euro-dollar market and the international monetary system commenced in late 1968, when the re-emergence of inflationary pressures in the US prompted the monetary authorities to reimpose fiscal and monetary restraint. It was intended that fiscal measures would be used to achieve a budget surplus whilst monetary restraint would be used to curb bank credit. The cornerstone of this latter policy was to be Regulation Q ceilings, although it was envisaged that the credit pressures of 1966 would not be repeated. Credit restraint was thus applied lightly at first -- the discount rate and prime rate were raised from 5¼% and 6½% to 5½% and 6¾% respectively on December 18th -- but as demand pressures began to intensify in the early months of 1969, the differential between secondary market CD rates and Regulation Q ceilings began to widen. The resulting attrition of CDs, as investors switched their maturing CDs into Treasury bills and commercial paper, subjected banks' reserves to increasing strains which were subsequently intensified by further attempts to contain inflationary pressures. Thus, despite official assurances that the Federal Reserve sought to avoid a repetition of the events of 1966, the reliance on monetary rather than fiscal policy and the measures which this entailed were clearly instrumental in exacerbating the reserve pressures which began developing in the early part of 1969: on April 4th the discount rate was raised from 5½% to 6%, followed almost immediately on April 17th by the raising of demand deposit reserve requirements from 17% to 17½%. In conjunction with other general contractionary measures, a policy was thus pursued which permitted US prime rates and prime commercial paper rates to reach historic peaks of 8½% and 8.65% in June and July respectively. The maximum rate payable on new issues of 90-day CDs, in contrast, remained at 6%, resulting in severe and sustained CD attrition (large CDs issued by large US commercial banks declined by more than half from $24.3 billion to $11.3 billion in the twelve months ending November 1969). The principal consequences of this attrition were reserve losses for the banking system as a whole and increases in weighted reserve requirements, since the substitution of commercial paper for CDs raised reserve requirements from 6% to 17½%.

This combination of reserve losses and increased weighted reserve requirements further intensified reserve pressures which banks attempted to mitigate by recourse to Federal funds, the liquidation of government securities, increased commercial paper issues by bank affiliates, reduced loan commitments and, finally and inevitably, by massive and sustained recourse to Euro-dollar borrowing -- banks' liabilities to overseas branches increased from $7 billion at the end of 1968 to a peak of $15 billion by November 1969 (table 5) -- the impact of which was experienced at both a US level, where it acted as a relief mechanism enabling individual banks to mitigate the contractionary effects of US monetary policy whilst also enabling banks collectively to achieve net reserve savings, and at an international level, where borrowings and their subsequent repatriations would, in a matter of months, destabilise both European capital markets and the international monetary system in general.

MECHANISMS AND BENEFITS OF US BANKS' EURO-DOLLAR BORROWING

The advantages of Euro-dollar borrowing for US banks assumed two basic forms:

Reserve-neutral Benefits

These benefits enabled individual banks to recoup reserve losses and effect borrowing cost reductions but did not extend net reserve savings to the banking system collectively:

Euro-dollar borrowing enabled banks with overseas branches to acquire deposits and hence reserves from banks both with and without overseas branches although, in the former case, to the extent that CD attrition was primarily concentrated on large commercial banks to whom, in turn, overseas branches principally belonged, banks were in effect only reacquiring their own reserves. In this respect the Euro-dollar market acted merely as a financial turntable, albeit one which individual banks could ill afford to ignore.

A second reserve-neutral benefit, separate and quite distinct from net reserve savings, involved the avoidance of increases in weighted reserve requirements resulting from the transfer of US CDs to the Euro-dollar market. By reacquiring these funds in the form of time deposits, banks were able to avoid the 17½% reserve requirement which Euro-dollar deposits would most likely have entailed. The scope for exploiting this facility -- and hence the impact of benefits arising from it -- was negligible, however, since there were few opportunities to attract Euro-dollars on a time deposit basis.

A third reserve-neutral benefit resulted from US banks' ability to exploit US and Euro-dollar interest rate differentials. Because of legal (FDIP), geographical and psychological impediments to the free flow of capital from the US to the Euro-dollar market, it was possible for US banks to secure marginal funds in the Euro-dollar market at rates higher than those prevailing in the US without having to pay these higher rates on total US funds. This enabled banks to sustain a level of assets higher than would have been sustainable in the absence of such deposit discrimination.

Fourthly, US banks were able to exploit a technical anomaly by which reserves could be secured for three days but at an equivalent one day's nominal cost. Referred to as "weekend borrowing" (although it applied to any period when money markets were closed), it resulted from the overnight delay in settling clearing house transactions. Banks borrowing Euro-dollars on Thursday for delivery on Friday could, by using clearing house cheques as payment on Friday, retain the reserves until the following Monday. Although interest rates generally adjusted to reflect these benefits, some measure of cost savings was nevertheless possible.

A final reserve-neutral benefit involved the sale of loans by US banks' head offices to their overseas branches. By requiring overseas branches to secure Euro-dollars to purchase head office loans, US banks were able to obtain additional funds for domestic purposes whilst maintaining foreign loan commitments within official restraint guidelines. Loan sales conducted on either a permanent or repurchase (cosmetic) basis thus represented a flexible and profitable technique for adjusting domestic reserve levels as well as loan portfolios.

Reserve-neutral benefits, therefore, enabled individual banks to recoup reserve losses, secure reserves at the expense of other banks and achieve borrowing cost savings. Unlike reserve-positive benefits, however, they did not enable the banking system collectively to achieve net reserve savings.

Reserve-positive Benefits

Reserve-positive benefits enabled the banking system as a whole to secure net reserve gains through direct borrowing initiatives and hence to achieve net increases in domestic lending activities:

The first such benefit involved the transformation (via the Euro-dollar market) of reserve-bearing deposits into reserve-free liabilities. This facility constituted the single most important aspect of Euro-dollar borrowing and resulted from the provisions of the Federal Reserve's Regulation M which distinguished, for reserve purposes, between deposits subject to conventional reserve requirements and liabilities due to banks' overseas branches which were classified as "other liabilities" and were consequently free from such requirements. Although no economic or financial distinction existed between deposits and borrowings, (the distinction was essentially legal, involving the subordination of creditors' in favour of depositors' claims in the event of a bank failure), the transformation of the former into the latter through Euro-dollar borrowing enabled banks individually and collectively to reduce required reserves, since a transfer of $100 from a US demand deposit to the Euro-dollar market and the reacquisition of this sum as Euro-dollar borrowings released $17.5 of reserves. It was this single, administratively-determined factor which accounted for the greater part of the phenomenal growth of Euro-dollar borrowing in 1969.

A second reserve-positive benefit exploited accounting anomalies and the provisions of the Federal Reserve's Regulation D to effect reserve savings through overnight Euro-dollar borrowing. These savings resulted from the one day's delay in cheque clearings and the accounting treatment of "Cash Items in the Process of Collection". A US bank requiring reserves on an overnight basis would instruct its overseas branch(es) to acquire Euro-dollars which would then be transferred to the account of the debtor US bank. Since this transaction would have involved a clearance delay, the recipient bank would have credited the cheque to an account designated "Cash Items in the Process of Collection", the contra entry to which would have been a liability to the bank's foreign branch. Collection items could be deducted from gross demand deposits to avoid the imposition of reserve requirements on borrowings before the actual reserves were received, but since the liability to the foreign branch was already reserve-free, the effect of this deduction was to achieve a net reduction in total deposits subject to reserves and hence to reduce already existing required reserves. By rolling over these loans, moreover, banks could create a semi-permanent pool of released reserves, the importance of which is indicated, as is the inhibiting effect exerted by the amendment of Regulation D in July 1969, by the fact that overnight dollar deposits reported by the foreign branches of US banks declined from 11% to 6% ($1.4 billion) of total deposits between June and August 1969.

A third and final benefit, but one which depended on the portfolio preferences of government debt holders and was therefore beyond the immediate individual or collective jurisdiction of banks, involved the transfer of receipts from the sale or redemption of government securities to the Euro-dollar market. Banks could thus improve their collective reserve position to the extent that Euro-dollar borrowing raised interest rates and induced a reallocation of existing or potential claims on the US government to the Euro-dollar market. (There can be no doubt that a substantial incentive existed for US government debt holders to transfer their assets to the Euro-dollar market, since the average closing monthly differential between three-month Euro-dollars and three-month US Treasury bills in favour of Euro-dollars exceeded three percentage points in 1969). A measure of the potential magnitude of the reserve gain which may have been realised is indicated by the change in US non-resident holdings of US Treasury obligations (bills, certificates and marketable and non-marketable bonds and notes), which declined by $1.9 billion in the first six months of 1969.

The quantifiable benefits of US banks' Euro-dollar borrowing depended largely on the original form in which the deposits appeared and on the nature of the Euro-dollar flows themselves. The replacing of domestic time deposits with reserve-free liabilities to foreign branches, for example, afforded minimal benefits of 38 basis points which represented the difference between the nominal (6%) and real (6.38%) cost of domestic time deposits.[1] Similar modest savings of 149 basis points, representing the difference between nominal (8.5%) and real (7.01%) prime rates, could be achieved by substituting reserve-free liabilities to foreign branches for domestic demand deposits.[2] Overnight Euro-dollars, however, conferred more substantial benefits, since such borrowing was not only reserve-free but also released $17.5 of reserves from existing demand deposit liabilities for every $100 borrowed. Funds thus secured offered a real prime rate of return, taking into account compensating balances, of more than 10%. Since Euro-dollar rates generally remained within a range of 10% - 11% in the second half of 1969, US banks were assured of a relatively stable and moderately-priced supply of short-term reserves. Yet even these cost differentials do not adequately reflect the advantages of Euro-dollar borrowing, for in periods of monetary restraint and reserve depletion, the longer-term benefits of avoiding portfolio sales and loan recalls may significantly outweigh the short-term marginal costs of securing additional reserves.

The Euro-dollar market did not prove of unmitigated benefit, however, for whilst it could confer substantial reserve savings it could also occasion deposit flows which undermined and at times even outweighed these reserve gains.

One such flow was the acquisition of Euro-dollars which had previously been held as demand deposits. This was costly for individual banks since it involved paying Euro-dollar rates for reserves which had previously been cost-free.

A second deposit flow occasioning reserve losses -- the avoidance of which frequently constituted the raison d'être of overseas branch borrowing -- involved inter-bank reserve losses resulting from the transfer of deposits from US banks to the overseas branches of US banks other than those in which the deposits were originally lodged. Whilst it might have been expected that banks would have recouped reserve losses through the normal course of trading activities, there was no guarantee that such gains would in fact be realised. It was this fear of net reserve losses which prompted US banks to secure deposits from overseas branches, thereby bidding up Euro-dollar rates and effectively converting low cost US deposits into relatively high cost (albeit reserve-free) liabilities to overseas branches. By thus acting as a turntable, the Euro-dollar market was trading released reserves against higher borrowing costs -- a trade-off which generally operated to the detriment of borrowing banks.

A third and final source of reserve pressure involved the financial disintermediation which occurred when deposits were transferred from US non-bank financial intermediaries to the Euro-dollar market. In such a situation not only did US financial liabilities decline and net reserve costs increase, but the banking system collectively experienced net reserve losses if, for example, deposits were "leaked" to the US government through purchases of new Treasury bills.

The question of whether these costs outweighed or were outweighed by the benefits of Euro-dollar borrowing may best be answered by reference to the liabilities of US banks in general and large New York City (NYC) banks in particular, since the latter experienced the severest attrition of CDs and consequently, because they had the readiest access to overseas facilities through foreign branches, made heaviest use of Euro-dollar borrowing. The Euro-dollar market's mitigating impact may most appropriately be assessed on the basis of loans, US Treasury securities and time and savings deposits, since relative changes in these instruments were most likely to have reflected NYC banks' ability to deflect or moderate the Federal Reserve's restraint programme. Details of these positions are illustrated in figure 3-1 (p. 35) which shows that:

Firstly, since NYC banks' share of total loans remained at a stable 15% between 1968 and 1970, Euro-dollar borrowing did not constitute a means by which these banks were able to increase their share of loan activity in relation to the banking system as a whole;

Secondly, although Euro-dollar borrowing did not allow NYC banks to increase their share of loans, it might have enabled them to maintain their share of loans by circumventing the need to re-establish reserve ratios through the liquidation at a loss of reserve bearing assets such as Treasury securities. If this had been the case, NYC banks might have been expected to increase their share of Treasury securities or alternatively, if the restraint programme had exerted a disproportionately contractionary impact on them, to maintain their share of securities. Changes in security shares do not reveal a discernible financing pattern, however, since the decrease in NYC banks' share of securities from 9% to 7% between the fourth quarter of 1968 and the second quarter of 1969 corresponded to an increase in liabilities to foreign branches from \$5.1 billion to \$9.3 billion, whilst the increase from 7% to 9% between the second and fourth quarters of 1969 corresponded to a relatively stable \$9 billion of liabilities to foreign branches, suggesting that Euro-dollar borrowing did not permit NYC banks to pursue a demonstrably beneficial Treasury securities policy;

Thirdly, the close correspondence between declines in NYC banks' time and savings deposits and increases in liabilities to overseas branches suggests that Euro-dollar borrowing was used extensively to recoup deposits, and hence reserves, lost through CD attrition.

These observations inevitably prompt the supplementary question of whether the Euro-dollar market was responsible for exacerbating CD losses or whether, in the market's absence, banks would have experienced even greater reserve depletions -- a question which may best be approached in terms of the market's overall impact:

Figure 3-1

SELECTED ASSETS AND LIABILITIES OF LARGE NEW YORK CITY BANKS AND TOTAL US BANKS 1966 - 1971

($ billions and %)

	LOANS		%	US TREASURY SECURITIES		%	TIME AND SAVINGS DEPOSITS		%	LIABILITIES TO FOREIGN BRANCHES		%
	NYC	Total		NYC	Total		NYC	Total		NYC	Total Large Banks	
1966 Q4	35.4	217.7	16	4.7	56.2	8	16.5	159.8	10	---	4.0	--
1967 Q4	38.0	236.0	16	5.5	62.5	9	19.1	183.8	10	3.4	4.2	81
1968 Q4	40.5	265.3	15	5.6	64.5	9	19.2	204.4	9	5.1	6.9	74
1969 Q1	40.6	265.0	15	4.2	58.5	7	16.6	203.2	8	6.9	9.6	72
Q2	42.8	283.9	15	4.0	54.0	7	14.4	200.8	7	9.3	13.3	70
Q2[1]	41.9	283.9	15	4.0	54.0	7	14.4	200.8	7	9.3	13.3	70
Q3	41.6	284.3	15	4.3	53.2	8	12.9	194.7	7	9.9	14.3	69
Q4	45.3	295.5	15	4.7	54.7	9	13.8	194.5	7	8.7	12.8	68
1970 Q1	41.9	288.2	15	4.2	51.5	8	14.1	196.9	7	8.1	11.9	68
Q2	41.2	296.1	14	4.0	51.6	8	13.7	205.0	7	8.1	12.2	66
Q3	43.1	301.5	14	4.8	55.8	9	17.7	221.6	8	6.9	9.7	71
Q4	44.3	313.3	14	5.6	61.7	9	19.2	233.1	8	5.2	7.7	68
1971 Q1	42.4	310.4	14	5.4	61.6	9	21.1	249.5	8	1.6	2.9	55
Q2	43.9	322.9	14	4.9	60.3	8	22.6	256.4	9	1.2	1.5	80
Q3	44.9	331.0	14	4.5	58.7	8	23.6	264.4	9	1.7	2.5	68
Q4	45.4	346.9	13	5.0	64.9	8	23.5	275.2	9	0.6	0.9	67

Source: Federal Reserve Bulletin, various issues

1. Break in series

Firstly, Euro-dollar borrowing did not enable banks with ready access to Euro-dollar borrowing to deflect contractionary pressures onto banks denied similar facilities;

Secondly, Euro-dollar borrowing was principally used to recoup reserve losses engendered by CD attrition, although the extent of CD causality is not readily determinable;

Thirdly, Euro-dollar borrowing enabled individual banks to effect reserve gains both "internally" and by attracting reserves from competing institutions.

The Euro-dollar market thus appears to have acted as an important source of individual reserve financing but only as a marginal source of collective reserve augmentation. Indeed, since a $17.5 reserve gain can hardly be expected to compensate for a $100 open market operations reserve loss, it is difficult to see how this could have been otherwise.

REGULATORY AMENDMENTS AND REASONS FOR DELAY

In the latter half of 1969, the US Federal Reserve effected three amendments to Regulations D and M in an attempt to curb both the high level of US banks' Euro-dollar borrowing and the destabilising repercussions ensuing from this borrowing:

Amendment to Regulation D, July 1969

With effect from July 31st 1969, Regulation D was amended to ensure that officers' cheques issued by a member bank or by (or on behalf of) a foreign branch of a member bank on an account maintained with a domestic office of the parent bank, were included by the member bank in deposits subject to reserves, thereby proscribing the reserve gains arising from the use of bills payable or "London" cheques.

Amendments to Regulation D and M, September 1969

Regulation M

Commencing October 16th 1969 and based on a four-week computational period effective September 4th 1969, US banks were required to maintain reserves of 10% of the amount by which balances due to overseas branches exceeded the corresponding daily average total for the four-week period ending May 28th 1969. Any reduction, moreover, in the level of such balances below the level prevailing in May 1969 (at which date balances amounted to approximately $10 billion for banks collectively) would automatically reduce the reserve-free base to the new borrowing level. Thus, from September onwards, not only were further Euro-dollar borrowings subject to a 10% reserve requirement but existing borrowings in excess of the $10 billion base level were also subject to reserves.

Commencing October 16th 1969 and based on a four-week computational period effective September 4th 1969, a 10% reserve requirement was imposed on the level by which banks' sales of assets to their foreign branches exceeded the corresponding daily average total for the four-week period ending May 28th 1969.

Commencing October 16th 1969 and based on a four-week computational period effective September 4th 1969, a 10% reserve requirement was imposed on the level by which US banks' overseas branches' claims on US residents exceeded the corresponding daily average total for the four-week period ending May 28th 1969. This amendment was effected to prevent US residents from circumventing domestic restraint policies by resorting to direct borrowing from US banks' overseas branches.

Regulation D

Commencing October 16th 1969 and based on a four-week computational period effective September 4th 1969, a 10% reserve requirement was imposed on US banks' daily average balances due to the overseas branches of other foreign banks. This amendment was effected to prevent US banks' circumventing the amendment to Regulation M for, although Euro-dollar borrowing from foreign banks was more expensive than borrowing from overseas branches and was consequently not widely resorted to, the imposition of a 10% reserve requirement would have narrowed the differential in favour of borrowing from overseas banks.

Excluded from these amendments were: (i) the liabilities of foreign banks' US branches and agencies to their overseas branches and head offices because of the need to maintain adequate reserves and working balances. This exclusion did not seriously undermine the efficacy of the amendments, however, since US branches were requested to exercise restraint in their lending to Federal member banks; (ii) US residents' borrowing from US banks' overseas branches undertaken to comply with FDIP requirements; and (iii) US residents' borrowing from foreign banks which were exempted because of jurisdictional and supervisory difficulties.

The effect of these amendments was to proscribe the collective reserve-positive benefits of Euro-dollar borrowing although, since banks could still improve their individual reserve positions, there was no immediate decline in overseas borrowings. The specific nature of these amendments, however, clearly demonstrated the Federal Reserve's ability to circumscribe US banks' mitigation of domestic restraint policies and hence to avert the destabilising repercussions of such borrowing.

This inevitably raises the question of why such measures were not effected sooner and why, in failing to do so, the Federal Reserve effectively acquiesced in the instability engendered by Euro-dollar borrowing? A number of explanations are possible:

The Federal Reserve might, for example, have sought to mitigate the contractionary impact of its restraint policy by permitting banks to resort to wholesale Euro-dollar borrowing. Had this been the case, however, it is not immediately apparent why the Federal Reserve should have resorted to measures which raised international interest rates and restrained overseas demand, especially at a time when the US was seeking to effect a substantial improvement in its balance of payments. Moreover, if the Federal Reserve had indeed sought to mitigate the contractionary impact of its restraint policy, it must be asked why such severe policies were pursued in the first instance or, if they had proved more contractionary than anticipated, why their impact had not been mitigated with appropriate domestic palliatives which would have avoided the international destabilisation engendered by Euro-dollar borrowing.

It is possible, too, that the US authorities sought to strengthen the role of the Euro-dollar market to enhance the importance and reputation of the dollar in the international monetary system. Since the rapid growth of the Euro-dollar market had been proceeding unabated, however, this explanation attracts only limited support.

Since IET and the FDIP had prompted US corporations and non-residents to resort to the Euro-dollar market for dollar financing, it might have been considered that an enlarged Euro-dollar market with greater flexibility would have further stimulated private dollar financing demands and hence increased private non-resident holdings of dollars. This explanation, in conjunction with the final explanation, namely that the Euro-dollar market was used to strengthen the dollar and improve the US official settlements balance, attracts considerable support. By fostering a climate in which US banks resorted to Euro-dollar borrowing, the Federal Reserve was able to force up Euro-dollar rates and channel official and private dollars into the Euro-dollar market. This improved the official settlements balance both directly -- by reducing US liabilities to foreign official agencies -- and indirectly -- by retaining in private form dollars which might otherwise have been sold to these agencies. Moreover, to the extent that dollars were not sold for domestic currencies and private transfers to the Euro-dollar market were financed out of non-dollar currencies, the dollar would have strengthened and liabilities to foreign official institutions reduced further. So it was that the dollar strengthened to a spot premium against several leading European currencies in the first half of 1969 and that an official settlements deficit of $3.4 billion in 1967 was transformed into official surpluses of $1.6 billion and $2.7 billion in 1968 and 1969 respectively, despite net liquidity deficits of $4.7 billion, $1.6 billion and $6.1 billion respectively for each of these years.

Explanations for the delay in effecting appropriate regulatory amendments thus range in nature from internal to external. The credibility of these explanations is similarly wide-ranging for on the one hand it cannot be seriously contended that the Federal Reserve was unaware of the serious international monetary dislocation its policies were creating, whilst on the other hand it is difficult to maintain that Euro-dollar borrowing was sanctioned to mitigate the repercussions of an excessively onerous domestic restraint policy, since simple palliatives were available which would have proved both more effective and less disruptive. Similar considerations apply to attempts to strengthen and broaden the Euro-dollar market and its operations. This effectively leaves the desire to strengthen the dollar and improve the official settlements balance as the only plausible explanation of the Federal Reserve's policies [3] -- policies which ultimately achieved their objectives but at great cost and disruption to the international monetary system.

The Federal Reserve's policy of operating interest rate ceilings whilst permitting US banks -- as late as August 1969 -- to supplement reserve shortfalls through Euro-dollar borrowing was thus inherently and demonstrably destabilising. It is difficult to escape the conclusion, therefore, that since regulatory amendments were not instigated prior to September 1969 because external balance of payments considerations pervaded domestic policy objectives, a charge of "dereliction of international financial responsibility" may be substantiated. To this extent the US authorities must accept their share of responsibility for the events which US banks' Euro-dollar borrowing and subsequent repatriations were to occasion both directly and indirectly.

THE FINANCING OF US BANKS' EURO-DOLLAR BORROWING

US banks' Euro-dollar borrowing exerted a major expansionary impact on the Euro-dollar market in 1969, with liabilities increasing by $19.3 billion to $46.2 billion, $11 billion of which was accounted for in the first six months of the year. Details of these changes are illustrated in figure 3-2 (p. 41), which shows that the whole of the market's increase in net liabilities exclusive of the US ($5.2 billion) was used in the provision of financing facilities ($6 billion) to support US banks' Euro-dollar borrowing. This raises the question of the source of this financing and whether or not it was created endogenously.

The distribution of inside area financing flows is illustrated in figure 3-3 (p. 42), which shows that flows were channelled to the US both directly and indirectly. Direct flows were recorded by most reporting countries, whilst indirect flows were principally channelled through

Figure 3-2

EXTERNAL DOLLAR POSITIONS OF REPORTING EUROPEAN BANKS
December 1968 - June 1969

($ billions)

		December 1968	June 1969	Ch
	Liabilities	22.7	32.3	-
EXLUDING US	Assets	19.7	24.1	+
	Net	- 3.0	- 8.2	-
	Liabilities	4.1	5.5	-
VIS-A-VIS US	Assets	10.7	18.1	+
	Net	+ 6.6	+12.6	+
	Liabilities	26.9	37.9	-
TIONS	Assets	30.4	42.2	+
	Net	+ 3.5	+ 4.3	+

<u>S Annual Report</u>, 1970

Figure 3-3

EXTERNAL NET DOLLAR POSITIONS OF REPORTING EUROPEAN BANKS
December 1968 - June 1969

($ millions)

	EXCLUDING US			VIS-A-VIS US			T	
	Dec 1968	June 1969	Change	Dec 1968	June 1969	Change	Dec 1968	
uxembourg	---	+ 180	+ 180	+ 150	+ 150	---	+ 150	+
	- 280	- 950	- 670	+ 670	+ 1080	+ 410	+ 390	+
	+ 510	+ 950	+ 440	+ 470	+ 540	+ 70	+ 980	+
	+ 430	+ 580	+ 150	+ 140	- 20	- 160	+ 570	+
nds	- 20	+ 50	+ 70	+ 30	+ 100	+ 70	+ 10	+
	+ 140	+ 120	- 20	+ 140	+ 110	- 30	+ 280	+
and	+1040	+ 1260	+ 220	+ 530	+ 530	---	+1570	+
	-4860	-10410	-5550	+4470	+10080	+5610	- 390	-
	-3040	- 8220	-5180	+6600	+12570	+5970	+3560	+

BIS Annual Report, 1970

the UK, whose $5.6 billion increase in net claims on the US -- representing 93% of the inside area's total $6 billion increase in net claims on the US -- was financed by $1.6 billion of net liabilities vis-à-vis other reporting countries. Of this $6 billion increase, $2.6 billion was provided by the inside reporting area itself, $2.1 billion of which was accounted for by non-resident holdings of European currencies (figure 3-4, p. 44). With the negligible exception of France and Italy, declines were recorded in net non-resident domestic currency liabilities of all reporting countries, indicating that the contractionary impact of US banks' Euro-dollar borrowing was partly transmitted to reporting European countries by outflows on external domestic currency accounts. (External non-dollar foreign currency positions showed little change in the first six months of 1969, with net assets of $0.3 billion changing to net liabilities of $0.4 billion).

A complete tabulation of the sources and uses of Euro-dollars in the first half of 1969 is provided in figure 3-5 (p. 45), in which it may be seen that the balance of net claims on the US ($3.4 billion) was financed by Canada ($0.7 billion), Other Europe ($0.4 billion) and the Rest of the World ($2.3 billion), indicating that the Euro-dollar market acted primarily as a conduit, channelling credits from the outside area to the US whilst supplying only a limited portion of the funds itself.

The question remains, however, of whether or not these Euro-dollar flows were financed endogenously. This may best be answered by a comparison of observed Euro-dollar financing flows and US payments data which, because of their emphasis on measures of external equilibria, must be reorganised to permit the identification of relevant flow data. This reorganisation is accomplished in figure 3-6 (p. 46), which illustrates principal component US dollar flows for the period December 1968 to June 1969. It may be seen from the figure that total net outflows amounted to $7.8 billion and were financed almost entirely by US banks' liabilities to overseas branches. These flows are illustrated schematically in figure 3-7 (p. 47), which shows that 94% ($7.3 billion) of US banks' liabilities to overseas banks was financed out of dollar flows emanating from the Euro-dollar market,

Figure 3-4

EXTERNAL NET DOMESTIC CURRENCY POSITIONS OF REPORTING EUROPEAN BANKS
December 1968 - June 1969

($ millions)

	December 1968	June 1969	Change
Belgium/Luxembourg	- 260	- 230	+ 30
France	- 310	- 360	- 50
Germany	-1530	- 740	+ 790
Italy	- 300	- 350	- 50
Netherlands	- 190	- 120	+ 70
Sweden	- 140	- 120	+ 20
Switzerland	- 600	+ 380	+ 980
UK	- 560	- 280	+ 280
TOTAL	-3890	-1820	+2070

Source: BIS Annual Report, 1970

Figure 3-5

NET EURO-DOLLAR POSITIONS
December 1968 - June 1969

($ billions)

	December 1968		June 1969		Change	
EURO-DOLLAR SOURCES						
Inside Area Banks	8.0		8.7		-0.7	
Inside Area Non-banks	5.2		8.1		-2.9	
TOTAL INSIDE AREA		13.2		16.8		- 3.6
Other Europe		1.9		2.1		- 0.2
US		3.2		4.4		- 1.2
Canada		1.3		2.3		- 1.0
Rest of World		5.4		7.9		- 2.5
TOTAL		25.0		33.5		- 8.5
EURO-DOLLAR USES						
Inside Area Banks	3.2		3.8		+0.6	
Inside Area Non-banks	4.7		5.1		+0.4	
TOTAL INSIDE AREA		7.9		8.9		+ 1.0
Other Europe		1.5		1.3		- 0.2
US		9.5		16.7		+ 7.2
Canada		0.9		1.2		+ 0.3
Rest of World		5.2		5.4		+ 0.2
TOTAL		25.0		33.5		+ 8.5
NET SOURCES/USES[1]						
Inside Area Banks	-4.8		-4.9		-0.1	
Inside Area Non-banks	-0.5		-3.0		-2.5	
TOTAL INSIDE AREA		- 5.3		- 7.9		- 2.6
Other Europe		- 0.4		- 0.8		- 0.4
US		+ 6.3		+12.3		+ 6.0
Canada		- 0.4		- 1.1		- 0.7
Rest of World		- 0.2		- 2.5		- 2.3
TOTAL		---		---		---

Source: BIS Annual Report, 1970

1. A minus sign indicates that the area is a net supplier of funds

Figure 3-6
SELECTED US BALANCE OF PAYMENTS DATA
December 1968 - June 1969[1]

($ billions)

Balance on Current Account	-0.8
Balance on Long-term Capital Account	-1.9
Increase in Claims on Foreigners	-0.6
Errors and Omissions	-1.4
Reduction in Liabilities to:	
Private Non-bank Foreigners	-0.2
Official Foreigners	-2.6
Increase in Reserve Assets	-0.3
TOTAL	-7.8
Financed by Increases in:	
Liabilities to Overseas Branches of US Banks	+7.7
Liabilities to Other Banks	+0.1
TOTAL	+7.8

Source: Survey of Current Business, June 1975

1. Data not seasonally adjusted

Figure 3-7

RECONCILIATION OF INTERNATIONAL DOLLAR FLOWS

December 1968 - June 1969

($ billions)

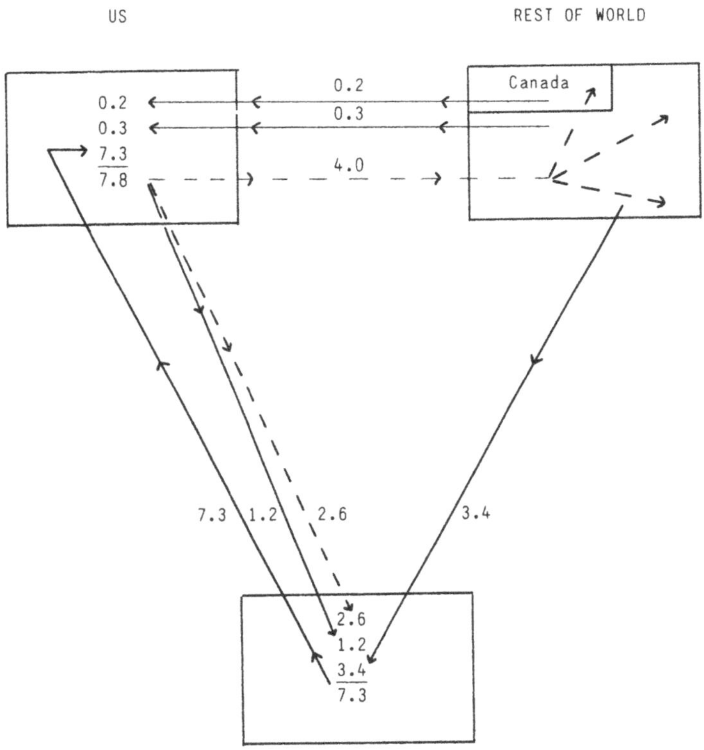

Solid lines depict direct claims on banks
Broken lines denote unidentified direct claims on banks and other dollar outflows

Sources: Survey of Current Business
BIS Annual Report
Bank of Canada Review

with the remaining $0.5 billion accounted for by flows from Canada ($0.2 billion) and the Rest of the World ($0.3 billion). The financing of these inflows was entirely accommodated out of dollar outflows from the US ($7.8 billion), of which $1.2 billion represented direct dollar claims on the Euro-dollar market and the balance of $6.6 billion direct and indirect claims, within which $4 billion flowed to the Rest of the World and $2.6 billion was absorbed by the Euro-dollar market. This $2.6 billion consisted of inside area bank (including central bank) and non-bank claims on inside area reporting banks originating from transactions such as dollar transfers from the US, export receipts, domestic currency conversions and non-domestic inside area currency conversions, and represented in essence the market's internal contribution to US banks' dollar financing.

The reconciliation of the various dollar flows financing US banks' dollar borrowing in the first half of 1969 indicates that US banks' overseas borrowing was financed with dollars created in the US and not in Europe and that the Euro-dollar market's US financing role was thus limited simply to the rechannelling of dollar claims to the US from both inside and outside the reporting area.

The conclusion may be drawn, therefore, that the financing of US banks' dollar borrowing was accommodated entirely out of existing dollar claims on the US, the majority of which were rechannelled to US banks through the Euro-dollar market either directly, from sources within the reporting area, or indirectly, from sources originating outside the reporting area. The process constituted none other than the placing of non-resident dollar claims on the US at the disposal of US banks for a specified period through the external medium of an off-shore dollar market and, to this extent, was merely a recycling operation precluding European dollar creation.

FINANCING REPERCUSSIONS

The principal repercussion of US banks' Euro-dollar borrowing was the transmission of US contractionary pressures to Europe, where measures to counteract capital outflows frequently conflicted with domestic policy objectives. An indication of the extent to which European monetary authorities were obliged to raise domestic interest rates to contain these outflows is given in table 6, which shows that substantial increases in European (and Canadian) central bank discount rates were effected in the first half of 1969 to counteract the effects of rising Euro-dollar rates, which accelerated from 7% in December 1968 to an historic peak of 13% by mid-June 1969 . These increases created serious policy conflicts for many European countries which were actively pursuing policies of low or stable interest rates. One such country was Italy, whose cheap money policy in pursuit of domestic expansion was undermined by arbitraged outflows to the Euro-dollar market. Similar constraints were imposed upon the UK where, despite increases in domestic interest rates to counteract increases in Euro-dollar rates, interest differentials in favour of Euro-dollars reached double figures by the third quarter of 1969. Other countries experienced similar problems: French franc investments, for example, became increasingly unattractive vis-à-vis the Euro-dollar, whilst a covered differential in favour of Euro-dollars emerged vis-à-vis even the Swiss franc. A major exception to this pattern, however, was Germany, which experienced a net capital inflow in the first nine months of 1969. Whilst this was accounted for in large measure by revaluationary expectations, it was also facilitated by a significant covered interest differential in favour of Deutsche Marks, the explanation for which lay not in the high level of German interest rates, but rather in the substantial forward premium on the Deutsche Mark. The rise in Euro-dollar rates thus proved a welcome development for the German authorities, since it narrowed interest differentials in favour of Deutsche Marks. This relief proved short-lived, however, for in the second quarter of 1969 the German authorities moved to sterilise a larger proportion of capital inflows for anti-inflationary purposes, with the result that increases in domestic interest rates counteracted the rise in Euro-dollar rates and further widened covered differentials in favour of Deutsche Marks.

The international financing repercussions of US banks' Euro-dollar borrowing were thus manifested in European capital outflows and increases in domestic interest rates --repercussions which might have been expected from any contractionary US monetary policy. The incidence of US Euro-dollar borrowing, however, served to magnify the impact of these repercussions. To the extent that US banks' Euro-dollar borrowing was administratively induced, therefore, the severe international monetary dislocation engendered in 1969 was almost entirely administrative in origin.

NOTES

1. The real cost of time deposits is:

$$\text{Real cost} = \frac{\text{Nominal Cost}}{1 - \text{Reserve Ratio}}.$$

With a time deposit ceiling rate of 6% and a reserve ratio of 6%, the real cost is 6.38%.

2. The real prime rate incorporates the percentage of demand deposits which have to be maintained as reserves and which cannot, therefore, be loaned out.

Real Prime Rate = Nominal Prime Rate (1-Reserve Ratio).

With a nominal prime rate of 8.5% and a reserve ratio of 17.5%, the real prime rate is 7.01%.

3. The extensive recourse to Euro-dollar borrowing in 1966 effectively precludes administrative delays as an explanation of the timing of regulatory amendments.

Chapter Four

REPATRIATED CAPITAL FLOWS AND THE EVENTS LEADING TO THE DOLLAR CRISIS OF 1971

US POLICY DEVELOPMENTS

In late 1969, the US authorities began to relax the monetary restraint which had occasioned US banks' Euro-dollar borrowing. With effect from January 21st 1970, Regulation Q ceilings were raised for the majority of time deposits and this, together with the accompanying increase in reserve availability, enabled banks to reduce their dependence on Federal funds and marginally unwind their Euro-dollar borrowings. This process was aided by the mid-year disclosure that the giant US Penn Central Transportation Company was insolvent, which prompted the authorities to make additional reserves available to the US banking system and to suspend, with effect from June 24th, Regulation Q ceilings on single maturity time deposits of $100,000 or more. This suspension proved of only passing interest to the Euro-dollar market, however, for although Regulation Q had once been one of the cornerstones of Euro-dollar activity, it had long since ceased to act as a necessary condition for Euro-dollar survival. The formal suspension of Q ceilings was nevertheless required to confirm this fact.

Monetary relaxation continued and indeed accelerated in the latter half of 1970, causing sharp declines in interest rates. Whereas the interest rate on new issues of three-month Treasury bills declined by just 90 basis points from an average 7.9% to 7% between January and June 1970, in the second half of the year it declined by 210 basis points to 4.9%. Similar declines were recorded for other market instruments, with the rate on three-month secondary market CDs, for example, exhibiting an almost uninterrupted decline from a peak of over 9% in January 1970 to a minimum of just under 4% by March 1971. The effect of this sustained and sharp decline in interest rates was to increase the viability of domestic CDs as a source of domestic financing for US banks, a fact which was reflected in an increase in major US commercial banks' large CDs from $10.5 billion in January 1970 to $27.2 billion by April 1971. As CDs increased in both availability and attractiveness, so Euro-dollar positions became relatively more expensive to finance, and the incentive for US banks to reduce their indebtedness to their overseas branches increased. Indeed the incentive was such that the repatriations which ensued proved even more dramatic than the original borrowings, for whereas the latter had commenced from a high borrowing base and had been effected over a longer period spanning as far back as the monetary restraint policy of 1966, the former were compressed into a period of a little over twelve months. Thus whereas it had taken from late 1965 to late 1969 for US banks to increase their liabilities to overseas branches from $1.5 billion to $15 billion, it took just eighteen months for these positions to be unwound to $1.5 billion by May 1971. In the light of the magnitude of these repatriations and the time scale involved, it was perhaps not altogether surprising that this unwinding should have proved highly destabilising both at a market level -- where the sustained inflow of a substantial volume of highly liquid funds subjected trading margins to intense pressure and converted a lenders' into a borrowers' market -- and at a wider international level -- where the ready availability of low cost funds occasioned European capital inflows which contributed to the Deutsche Mark and dollar crises of 1971.

The instability occasioned by Euro-dollar repatriations may be attributed in large measure to the Federal Reserve's failure to implement adequate measures to limit Euro-dollar repatriations and the resultant high level of international liquidity. The principal measures effected were:

Firstly, Regulation M was amended to raise reserve requirements on US banks' liabilities to their overseas branches from 10% to 20%. With effect from January 7th 1971, US banks were required to maintain reserves of 20% of the amount by which the daily average total of balances due to overseas branches over the four-week computational period commencing November 26th 1970 exceeded the corresponding daily average total for the computational period ending November 25th 1970 or (and this was the sting in the amendment's tail) the lowest corresponding daily average total for any computational period beginning after November 25th, whichever amount was the lower. Lest the logic of increasing reserve requirements on liabilities which exceeded a reserve-free base at a time when it was desired to restrain Euro-dollar repatriations is not immediately apparent, it may be noted that the object of the amendment was to automatically reduce the reserve-free base as repatriations progressed and hence, with a higher reserve requirement of 20%, to increase the cost of future borrowings. Thus with each new reduced level of liabilities to foreign branches, the cost of future borrowings was correspondingly increased. Not surprisingly, perhaps, the amendment was hardly a success for, with the steep decline in domestic interest rates, it was inevitable that US banks would heavily discount the future cost of Euro-dollar borrowing in terms of maintaining existing positions, and hence continue -- if not accelerate-- their Euro-dollar repatriations. Consequently between the end of October 1970 (when the amendment might be expected to have first exerted an impact) and April 1971, US banks' liabilities to their overseas branches declined from $9.3 billion to $2.5 billion (table 5).

The second measure, which was designed to complement the amendment to Regulation M, involved a special series of Treasury and Export-Import (Exim) Bank securities issued to US banks' overseas branches in an attempt to absorb the substantial liquidity which was flooding the international monetary system. The first $1.5 billion of 6% Exim Bank securities were issued in January and February 1971, followed by a further $1.5 billion of Treasury issues in April. The certificates remained in existence until the suspension of convertibility in August 1971, when they were discontinued and outstanding securities permitted to mature. The securities proved of only limited success, however, for whilst they absorbed liquidity which would otherwise have been dissipated into the international monetary system, it is doubtful whether this absorption exerted other than a marginally ameliorative impact when compared to the $10 billion of disposable liquidity which US banks injected into the international monetary system between November 1969 and the Deutsche Mark crisis of May 1971.

Just as the instability of 1969 had been largely attributable to US policy developments, so the dislocation subsequently engendered by US banks' Euro-dollar repatriations may be attributed to the US authorities' failure to effect appropriate preventative measures in adequate time. The situation was exacerbated, however, by a number of ancillary factors, most important of which was the international incompatibility of domestic policy objectives.

INCOMPATIBILITY OF DOMESTIC POLICY OBJECTIVES

Just as the rise in European interest rates occasioned by US banks' Euro-dollar borrowing in 1969 had conflicted with domestic policy objectives, so the subsequent decline in interest rates necessitated by the need to discourage unwanted capital inflows resulting from Euro-dollar repatriations caused similar conflicts which were largely resolved by discounting external constraints and allocating priority to domestic policy objectives. The resultant heavy capital inflows not only undermined domestic economic stability but also destabilised the international monetary order -- a process which culminated in the two exchange crises of 1971. Since Germany found itself at the centre of this conflict and since the May 1971 exchange crisis was centred on the Deutsche Mark, analysis of the incompatibility of domestic policy objectives will be focused on German policy developments and associated capital inflows.

Although the majority of European economies were cyclically lagging behind the US in early 1970 and were therefore resisting the need to relax monetary restraint, the overwhelming necessity of such policy changes (despite the continuing need to curb inflation) eventually persuaded European authorities to comply with external policy requirements. The principal exception to this was Germany, where the priority accorded monetary policy as an anti-inflationary weapon caused increases rather than decreases in domestic interest rates. In marked contrast to other European countries, therefore, Germany engineered further increases in short-term rates -- over and above the four percentage point increase recorded in 1969 -- to a peak of 9½% in the second quarter of 1970. This further widened the differential between German and Euro-dollar interest rates and, together with the increased availability of Euro-dollar deposits resulting from US repatriations, enhanced the profitability of both arbitraged and direct-borrowing inflows into Germany.

The incentive created for such flows is illustrated in figure 4-1 (p. 56), which depicts Deutsche Mark and Euro-dollar interest rates and attendant covered differentials for the period January 1970 to June 1971. The figure shows that uncovered three-month domestic Deutsche Mark deposits consistently yielded a higher return than comparable Euro-dollar deposits between March 1970 and April 1971 whilst, except for the second quarter of 1970, covered differentials also remained in favour of Deutsche Marks with spreads frequently exceeding 100 basis points. Even more pronounced, moreover, was the substantial differential between Deutsche Mark and Euro-dollar prime lending rates, which remained permanently in favour of the latter between June 1970 and April 1971.

The German authorities thus contributed to a situation in which substantial capital inflows -- both internally and externally initiated -- were only to be expected. Such inflows were indeed recorded, with German external corporate short-term liabilities increasing by a dollar equivalent of $1.9 billion in 1970 and a further $1.9 billion in the first five months of 1971. Similar increases were recorded in German banks' gross external liabilities, which increased by $2.3 billion in 1970, approximately $1.5 billion of which was denominated in Deutsche Marks. These flows contributed to a substantial $7.2 billion increase in German dollar reserves in 1970, financed in large measure by direct and indirect dollar inflows from the Euro-dollar market. (Surpluses on current, long-term capital and unclassifiable transactions accounts were insufficient to finance more than a modest $1.6 billion increase in reserves). German reserve increases resulting from arbitraged and direct borrowing inflows were a response, therefore,

Figure 4-1

THREE-MONTH DEUTSCHE MARK AND EURO-DOLLAR DEPOSIT INTEREST RATES AND COVERED DIFFERENTIALS; AND DEUTSCHE MARK AND EURO-DOLLAR PRIME LENDING RATES
January 1970 - June 1971

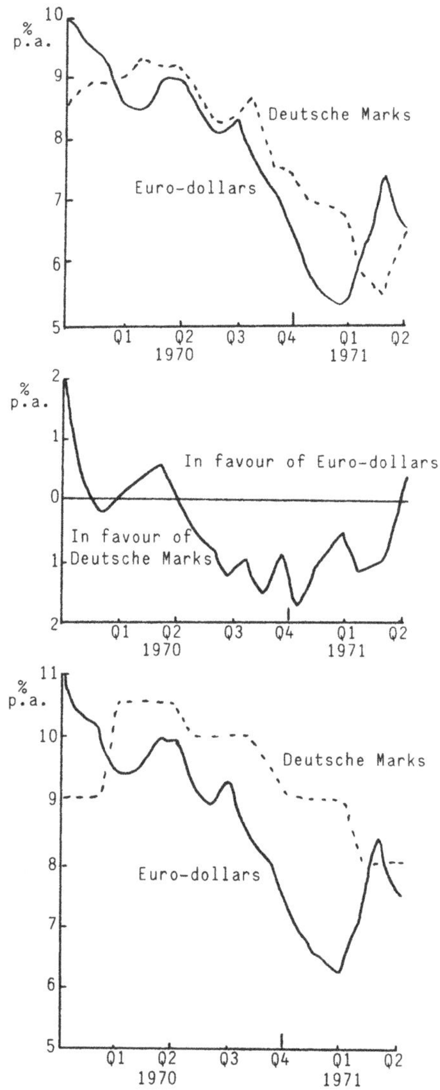

Three-month Deposit Rates

Covered Three-month Deposit Rate Differentials

Prime Lending Rates

Sources: IMF Annual Report, 1971
World Financial Markets, July 1971

to administratively created differentials and hence to deliberate policy decisions. Whether by choice or by miscalculation (and with the aid of hindsight it appears to have been the latter), the German authorities engineered a situation in which heavy and sustained capital inflows could hardly fail to have been generated. To the extent that these flows, through the destabilisation and reserve augmentation engendered, contributed to the events of May 1971, the German authorities must accept a measure of direct responsibility for the May Deutsche Mark crisis and indirectly, therefore, for the dollar crisis of 1971.

The incompatibility of domestic policy objectives and the reserve augmentation engendered by unwanted capital inflows represented, in essence, nothing more than the transition from the Euro-dollar market's temporary private financing of the US payments deficits of 1968 and 1969 through US banks' Euro-dollar borrowing to the permanent official financing of these deficits through official absorption of unwanted capital inflows. The destabilising repercussions of this financing were exacerbated, however, by the private and official funds which were drawn to the market but which, in differing circumstances, might have remained in non-volatile non-Euro-dollar form such as US Treasury obligations, and by the relatively short period into which this transition was compressed as well as the speed with which it was effected The US authorities' failure to implement appropriate preventative measures prior to the second half of 1969 and their corresponding failure to reduce the speed of Euro-dollar repatriations in 1970/71, together with the German authorities' failure to pursue domestic policies which did not provide a ready outlet for these funds thus permitted a highly unstable situation to develop which was to culminate in the Deutsche Mark crisis of May 1971.

THE DEUTSCHE MARK CRISIS

The May 1971 currency crisis was principally centred on the Deutsche Mark, whose strength was matched only by the weakness of the dollar. Just as German external corporate short-term liabilities and official dollar reserves had continued to increase in the first quarter of 1971, so the US net liquidity deficit had increased to a seasonally adjusted $3 billion over the same period, only $300 million of which was financed by increases in US banks' liabilities to foreign banks other than overseas branches. Together with the continuing high level of US banks' Euro-dollar repatriations, these flows contributed to an acceleration of the US official settlements deficit to a seasonally adjusted $5.9 billion in the first quarter of 1971.

The situation at the beginning of April was thus unstable and indeed continued to deteriorate throughout the month, with the Bundesbank purchasing approximately $3 billion through spot and forward support operations. It was not until the closing days of April, however, that the crisis proper developed, prompted largely by the recommendation of German research institutes that internal and external equilibrium should be restored through the floating of the Deutsche Mark and by the disclosure that the EEC Council of Ministers was considering the possibility of increased flexibility between European currencies and the dollar. Following the absorption of $1 billion on Monday May 3rd and Tuesday May 4th, and an estimated $1 billion in the first hour of trading on Wednesday 5th, the Bundesbank withdrew support from the dollar and the exchange markets were closed. Similar closures were initiated by the authorities of other leading European currencies to which exchange pressures had spread. When the markets reopened on Monday May 10th, the Deutsche Mark and the Dutch guilder were floating, and the Austrian schilling and Swiss franc had been revalued by 5.05% and 7.07% respectively.

The role of the Euro-dollar market in the financing of this crisis may be examined in terms of three major financing indicators:

Interest Rate Changes

Changes in Euro-dollar bid and offer rates for the period April - September 1971 are illustrated in figure 4-2 (p. 60), which shows that in the period leading up to the May crisis, short-term interest rates remained comparatively stable. Until the end of April, interest rates remained relatively trendless and, even after the buildup of speculative pressures on May 3rd, a one-eighth percentage point decline in one-month bid and offer rates failed to point towards any major trend. Significantly, it was not until after the Bundesbank withdrew its support and exchange markets were officially closed that interest rates responded to financing pressures, with call and seven-day interest rates rising to double figures, at which level they remained during the following week. Since exchange dealings continued on an unofficial basis after the markets were closed, this increase would suggest that short-term deposits were withdrawn and credits sought for speculative purposes after it had become evident that selected revaluations were imminent. To the extent that increased Euro-dollar rates reflected increased Euro-dollar financing demands, therefore, the greater part of the market's contribution to capital flows appears to have been concentrated on the period following the closure of the foreign exchange markets.

Changes in Reporting Positions

A second indicator of the Euro-dollar market's financing contribution embraces changes in positions reported by inside area banks and the overseas branches of US banks. Changes in aggregate market positions are illustrated in tables 7(i) - 7(iii), which indicate that during the second quarter of 1971 increases in dollar claims on both banks and non-banks were comparable to those recorded for immediately preceding quarters. The pattern relating to changes in dollar liabilities is less clearly defined, however, for although liabilities to non-banks declined by $210 million in the second quarter of 1971, this reduction must be seen within the context of an intermittently declining trend dating back to the second quarter of 1970. Nevertheless, to the extent that a decline in liabilities to non-banks was recorded (liabilities to banks increased by $2.5 billion), this would be consistent with the withdrawal of deposits for speculative financing purposes and with the non-depositing of dollars for similar objectives, although this latter function may hardly be considered a Euro-dollar financing role.

Sectoral changes in Euro-dollar flows are provided by the dollar positions of US banks'

Figure 4-2

EURO-DOLLAR BID AND OFFER RATES

April 2nd - September 3rd 1971

(% p.a.)

	CALL	7 DAYS	1 MONTH
d Apr	$4\frac{5}{8}$ - $5\frac{1}{8}$	$4\frac{3}{4}$ - $5\frac{1}{4}$	---
h Apr	$5\frac{1}{4}$ - $6\frac{1}{4}$	$5\frac{1}{4}$ - $6\frac{1}{4}$	---
h Apr	$4\frac{3}{8}$ - $4\frac{7}{8}$	$4\frac{1}{2}$ - $5\frac{1}{8}$	$5\frac{3}{8}$ - $5\frac{7}{8}$
d Apr	$4\frac{1}{4}$ - 5	$4\frac{3}{8}$ - $5\frac{3}{4}$	$5\frac{1}{4}$ - $5\frac{3}{4}$
h Apr	$4\frac{3}{4}$ - $5\frac{3}{8}$	$4\frac{7}{8}$ - $5\frac{1}{2}$	$5\frac{5}{8}$ - $6\frac{1}{8}$
d May	$4\frac{3}{4}$ - $5\frac{3}{8}$	$4\frac{7}{8}$ - $5\frac{1}{2}$	$5\frac{1}{2}$ - 6
h May	$4\frac{7}{8}$ - $5\frac{3}{8}$	5 - $5\frac{3}{4}$	$5\frac{5}{8}$ - $6\frac{1}{8}$
h May	$5\frac{1}{4}$ - 10	$5\frac{1}{2}$ - 10	$6\frac{3}{4}$ - $7\frac{1}{4}$
h May	11 - 13	11 - 13	$7\frac{3}{4}$ - $8\frac{3}{8}$
h May	8 - 10	8 - 10	$7\frac{1}{2}$ - 8
h May	9 - 11	9 - 11	$7\frac{3}{8}$ - $7\frac{7}{8}$
h May	9 - 11	9 - 11	$7\frac{3}{4}$ - $8\frac{1}{4}$
h May	$7\frac{1}{4}$ - $9\frac{1}{2}$	$7\frac{3}{8}$ - $9\frac{1}{2}$	7 - $7\frac{1}{2}$
h May	6 - 7	$6\frac{1}{4}$ - $7\frac{1}{4}$	7 - $7\frac{1}{2}$

	$5\frac{1}{4} - 6\frac{1}{4}$	$5\frac{1}{2} - 6\frac{1}{2}$	$6\frac{5}{8} - 7\frac{1}{8}$
	$5\frac{1}{4} - 6\frac{1}{4}$	$5\frac{1}{2} - 7$	$6\frac{3}{8} - 7\frac{1}{8}$
	$7\frac{7}{8} - 8\frac{3}{8}$	$7\frac{3}{4} - 8\frac{1}{4}$	$7\frac{1}{2} - 8$
e	$5\frac{3}{4} - 6\frac{1}{4}$	$6 - 6\frac{1}{2}$	$7\frac{1}{8} - 7\frac{5}{8}$
e	$5\frac{1}{4} - 5\frac{3}{4}$	$5\frac{3}{8} - 5\frac{7}{8}$	$6\frac{7}{8} - 7\frac{3}{8}$
e	$4\frac{1}{4} - 5$	$4\frac{1}{2} - 5\frac{1}{8}$	$6\frac{5}{8} - 7\frac{1}{8}$
e	$6\frac{1}{4} - 6\frac{3}{4}$	$6\frac{3}{4} - 7\frac{1}{4}$	$6\frac{3}{8} - 6\frac{7}{8}$
y	$4\frac{1}{4} - 5\frac{1}{4}$	$4\frac{1}{2} - 5\frac{1}{8}$	$5\frac{7}{8} - 6\frac{3}{8}$
y	$5\frac{1}{8} - 5\frac{5}{8}$	$5\frac{1}{4} - 5\frac{3}{4}$	$5\frac{7}{8} - 6\frac{3}{8}$
y	$5\frac{1}{4} - 5\frac{7}{8}$	$5\frac{3}{8} - 5\frac{7}{8}$	$6 - 6\frac{1}{2}$
y	$5\frac{1}{4} - 5\frac{3}{4}$	$5\frac{3}{8} - 6\frac{1}{2}$	$6 - 6\frac{1}{2}$
y	$6\frac{1}{4} - 6\frac{3}{4}$	$6\frac{3}{8} - 6\frac{7}{8}$	$6\frac{3}{8} - 6\frac{7}{8}$
	$6 - 6\frac{5}{8}$	$6\frac{1}{8} - 6\frac{3}{4}$	$6\frac{5}{8} - 7\frac{1}{8}$
	$6\frac{1}{4} - 6\frac{3}{4}$	$6\frac{3}{8} - 6\frac{7}{8}$	$6\frac{7}{8} - 7\frac{3}{8}$
	$6\frac{1}{2} - 7\frac{3}{4}$	$7 - 7\frac{3}{4}$	$7\frac{1}{4} - 7\frac{3}{4}$
	$8 - 9\frac{1}{8}$	$8\frac{1}{2} - 9\frac{1}{8}$	$8 - 8\frac{1}{2}$
	$8 - 9$	$8 - 8\frac{1}{2}$	$7\frac{5}{8} - 8\frac{1}{8}$
	$7\frac{1}{2} - 8\frac{1}{8}$	$7\frac{3}{4} - 8\frac{1}{4}$	$7\frac{5}{8} - 8\frac{1}{8}$
	*	---	$8\frac{1}{2} - 9$
	---	---	$8\frac{1}{2} - 9$

Figure 4-2 (cont'd)

	CALL	7 DAYS	1 MONTH
Aug	---	---	$8\frac{1}{2}$ - 9
Aug	---	---	10 - 11
Aug	---	---	$9\frac{3}{4}$ - 11
Aug	---	---	9 - 10
Aug	8 - 9	8 - 10	$8\frac{5}{8}$ - $9\frac{1}{8}$
Aug	$8\frac{1}{4}$ - $9\frac{1}{4}$	$8\frac{1}{2}$ - $9\frac{1}{2}$	$9\frac{1}{4}$ - $9\frac{3}{4}$
Sep	$7\frac{7}{8}$ - 9	$8\frac{1}{8}$ - $9\frac{1}{4}$	$9\frac{1}{4}$ - $9\frac{3}{4}$

inal bid rates of 22% reported at one point

Financial Times, various issues

foreign branches which, although including banks located outside the reporting area, may nevertheless be used as a suitable proxy for component flows contained within aggregate market data. Details of these changes are provided in table 8, which reveals that liabilities to foreign non-banks and foreign official institutions declined by $182 million and increased by $420 million respectively in April -- positions which were reversed in the following month, with liabilities increasing by $18 million and decreasing by $324 million respectively. These changes would be compatible with a limited private Euro-dollar financing role and the subsequent unwinding of speculative currency conversions. Changes in dollar claims do not fully accord with such a pattern, however, for the $1443 million increase in claims on banks reported in March was recorded too early to be of direct speculative importance, whilst increases reported in April and May were not inconsistent with those recorded in other periods, although it should be noted that claims on "other" increased by $1535 million in April. In conjunction with data on liabilities and aggregate market positions, therefore, these changes would support the existence of a direct, albeit limited, Euro-dollar financing role.

Changes in US Payments Data

The third and final financing indicator relates not to the Euro-dollar market directly but rather to changes in US payments data. These changes are of importance not only because they provide an indication of alternative financing sources, but also because they offer a means of corroborating the extent of the Euro-dollar market's financing commitment. Thus if it can be shown that a substantial increase in US capital outflows corresponded to increased pressure on the Deutsche Mark, this would serve to endorse the conclusions relating to a limited Euro-dollar financing role.

US capital flows may assume a variety of forms differing in both magnitude and financing impact:

At times of speculative pressure on the dollar, it might be expected that foreign private holdings of US Treasury bonds and notes and corporate securities would be liquidated to effect conversions into stronger currencies.

This does not appear to have occurred to any significant extent in the second quarter of 1971, however, with holdings of bonds and notes declining by a negligible $29 million and holdings of corporate securities actually increasing by $8 million in April and May. US holdings of foreign securities increased by a similarly modest $248 million over the same period.

US banks' liabilities to non-official foreigners constitute the most direct form of currency financing, since dollar sales must necessarily be effected with claims on the US banking system. Neither quarterly nor monthly changes in liabilities, however, reveal any significant financing patterns:

-- liabilities to non-monetary international and regional organisations increased by $196 million in the second quarter of 1971, of which increases in April and May accounted for $163 million and $48 million respectively;

-- liabilities to non-banks declined by $121 million in the second quarter of 1971, an increase of $51 million and a decrease of $87 million being recorded in April and May respectively;

-- liabilities to banks, excluding the repayment of Euro-dollar borrowings, increased by $1.5 billion in the second quarter of 1971, of which $4 million and $1.2 billion were recorded in April and May respectively.

A further source of financing embraces bank reported short-term claims such as dollar loans to foreign banks and non-banks, "other" claims (principally claims on US foreign branches and US agencies'/branches' overseas head offices) and claims denominated in foreign currencies. Examination of changes in these positions for April and May reveals a more discernible financing pattern: claims on banks and non-banks increased by a combined $319 million; "other" claims increased by $322 million; and claims denominated in foreign currencies increased by $72 million, within which foreign currency deposits increased by $110 million. The total increase amounted to $713 million which, in conjunction with the increase in the US errors and omissions item, is suggestive of a more significant financing role.

The penultimate source of financing embraces increases in short-term liquid claims reported by US non-banks. On an aggregated quarterly basis these claims reveal little of consequence, since total claims increased by a mere $8 million in the second quarter of 1971. On a disaggregated monthly basis, however, a more discernible financing pattern emerges, with total short-term liquid claims reported by large non-banking concerns increasing by $82 million in April and May 1971. Of greater import was the fact that, within this total, short-term liquid claims denominated in foreign currencies increased by $134 million. This increase is of interest not only because it indicates conclusively that identifiable US dollar outflows were used to effect increases in foreign currency deposits, but also because it suggests, in conjunction with the substantial increase in US errors and omissions, that a significant volume of dollars may have been transferred abroad to effect foreign currency conversions whilst remaining statistically unidentified in US payments data.

The final and most potent financing source embraces the net errors and omissions item in US balance of payments data. This item consists essentially of unrecorded capital flows and its significance derives not only from the magnitude of the outflows involved but also from the close correspondence between increases in these outflows and currency instability. Whereas the errors and omissions outflow amounted to an average annual $233 million in the latter half of the sixties (an inflow of $82 million if the 1969 outflow of $1.5 billion is excluded) and to $476 million in 1970, the outflow accelerated to a substantial $2.3 billion in the second quarter of 1971 -- an outflow which was repeated for the third quarter of 1971 and the first quarter of 1973, quarters which were also characterised by periods of intense speculative activity. This $2.3 billion would have been capable of accommodating a large proportion of the net dollar conversions effected during this quarter.

A distillation of the evidence relating to both Euro-dollar and US flow data thus indicates that the Euro-dollar market contributed to the financing of speculative currency conversions but that this role appears to have been of limited consequence. US flow data, in contrast, reveal not only that there was an identifiable increase in foreign claims reported by US banks and non-banks in April and May 1971 -- proving conclusively, in the latter case, that US non-banks increased their holdings of foreign currency deposits -- but also that there was a quantum increase in errors and omissions amounting to $2.3 billion in the second quarter of the year. It may be concluded, therefore, that whilst the Euro-dollar market contributed directly to the financing of the May Deutsche Mark crisis, this role proved of only limited significance and that the predominant source of financing was US capital outflows.

THE PROLIFERATION OF CAPITAL CONTROLS

Although the floating of the Deutsche Mark and guilder and the revaluation of the Swiss franc and Austrian schilling restored stability to the international monetary system, the Deutsche Mark crisis was not without consequence for the longer-term development of the Euro-dollar market, for as a direct result of both the crisis itself and the events leading up to it there ensued a proliferation of capital controls and monetary restrictions which, if not inimical to the expansion of the Euro-dollar market, at least served to reorientate its growth and development. These measures assumed the form of restrictions on the placing of official deposits in the market and restrictions designed to curb unwanted capital inflows:

The Group of Ten Agreement

Foremost amongst the individual restrictions introduced in the first half of 1971 was the agreement reached in June amongst the governors of the central banks of the Group of Ten to suspend further deposits in the Euro-dollar market and to withdraw such funds when market conditions permitted. The agreement constituted the first co-ordinated attempt to curb and, where possible, reduce Euro-dollar activity and reflected the increasing realisation that central banks' Euro-dollar depositing could exacerbate exchange rate instabilities by providing the resources necessary to finance successive rounds of currency speculation. The immediate impact of the agreement was limited, however, for whilst industrial countries' identified holdings of Euro-dollars declined by $1.4 billion in 1971, this decline was more than offset by an increase of $2.2 billion in other countries' identified holdings of Euro-dollars (table 4). The agreement's longer-term impact was also limited, not because of any inherent failure to implement its agreed provisions, but rather because the intensification of capital controls in European capital markets restricted the investment of international reserves in the national markets of the currencies concerned and hence diverted reserves to the Euro-dollar market which offered higher returns than those obtainable in the US.

Notwithstanding these limitations, however, the agreement was significant because it reflected a transition from a climate of relative capital mobility to one in which new controls were introduced and existing controls strengthened in increasingly futile attempts to correct what ostensibly were temporary exchange rate imbalances but which, in reality, had developed into fundamental payments disequilibria. Thus not only did the agreement represent the first concerted attempt to regulate and curb Euro-dollar activity -- a significant departure from the practices of previous years when extensive recourse was made to Euro-dollars for both official and officially sanctioned private purposes -- but it also constituted part of a more comprehensive series of measures designed to curb unwanted capital inflows and hence indirectly circumscribe Euro-dollar activity.

National Capital Controls

The proliferation and intensification of national capital controls early in 1971 signalled the transition from a period of deflationary capital outflows to one in which excessive inflows were threatening to dislocate European economies and exacerbate inflationary pressures. The controls were thus designed not so much to directly inhibit Euro-dollar borrowing or curb Euro-dollar activity per se, but rather to curb unwanted capital inflows. In essence they were intended to disfranchise domestic European markets as profitable outlets for Euro-dollar funds. The major provisions of the controls as they affected the leading industrial countries were:

Germany

The payment of interest on non-resident domestic and foreign currency deposits and the acquisition of selected categories of domestic financial assets by non-residents were prohibited. Average and marginal reserve ratios on non-resident liabilities were also raised.

The Netherlands

The payment of interest on selected non-resident guilder demand deposits (with maturities of 30 days or less) was prohibited.

Belgium/Luxembourg

The official and free franc markets were separated completely and restrictions were imposed on both the opening of new deposit accounts by non-residents and the payment of interest on existing accounts.

France

Reserve requirements on non-resident liabilities were increased and the payment of interest on deposits of 90 days or less was prohibited.

Italy

No new restrictions were announced.

Switzerland

No major changes in exchange restrictions were announced.

Japan

Restrictions were imposed on residents' foreign currency borrowing for domestic use and on non-resident purchases of government securities.

The UK

Foreign currency borrowing for domestic use was restricted to periods of five years or longer and the exchange guarantee on foreign currency borrowing by nationalised industries and local authorities was restricted to loans with maturities of ten years or longer.

The short-term consequence of these controls was to reduce the opportunities for the profitable deployment of Euro-dollars, and this, together with the increased liquidity resulting from US banks' Euro-dollar repatriations and US payments deficits, served to transform the Euro-dollar market from a lenders' into a borrowers' market. The longer-term consequence of this transition was to reorientate the market towards less-developed countries and towards marginal borrowers who in previous years might have found accommodation in the market either difficult or else comparatively expensive.

The impact of these controls was not confined to the Euro-dollar market, however, for at a more general level the controls seriously undermined the urgency with which international payments disequilibria had to be corrected and consequently intensified the magnitude and severity of the adjustment process which eventually and inevitably had to come.

Chapter Five

THE 1971 DOLLAR CRISIS

THE ONSET OF THE CRISIS

Despite the currency realignment which followed the Deutsche Mark crisis and the intensification of measures to curb destabilising capital flows, an atmosphere of uncertainty pervaded the international currency markets in the summer of 1971. The US merchandise trade balance swung from a surplus of $160 million in March to a deficit of $365 million by June, whilst the seasonally adjusted deficit on current and long-term capital account deteriorated from $1.7 billion to $3.2 billion between the first and second quarters of the year. These flows contributed to an official settlements deficit of $12.1 billion in the first half of 1971 and further undermined confidence in the dollar which was traded at a spot discount against virtually every major trading currency. With little prospect of an improvement in the US balance of payments through "conventional" remedies, some form of discrete adjustment became increasingly inevitable. This was duly prompted by a US Congressional Sub-committee report (the Reuss report) which cautioned that conventional measures could be expected to prove of limited success in the restoration of payments equilibrium and that consequently, in the absence of a general currency realignment, there might be no option but to suspend convertibility of the dollar. Following the report's publication, a flight from the dollar developed and steadily gained momentum. During the week commencing Monday August 9th, international dollar reserves increased by $3.7 billion ($1.7 billion of which was accounted for by Switzerland), whilst stabilisation measures resulted in a $1.2 billion decline in US reserve assets. By the end of the week it had become apparent that the situation was untenable and, on Sunday August 15th, President Nixon announced the suspension of dollar convertibility and the imposition of a 10% import surcharge. "Bretton Woods", in all but name, had collapsed.

When the exchange markets reopened on Monday August 23rd, virtually every major industrial currency, with the exception of the Japanese Yen, was floating. Four months later, on December 18th, the Smithsonian Agreement concluded a 7.9% devaluation of the dollar, equivalent to the raising of the official gold price from $35 to $38 an ounce.

The August dollar crisis, representing the partial collapse of the existing financial order constructed on fixed exchange rates and dollar convertibility, was the single most important monetary event of 1971 and one of the most significant monetary developments of the post-war era. Of interest, therefore, is the existence of a potential Euro-dollar financing role seen within the context of a $6 billion increase in international exchange reserves in the two weeks preceding the closure of the foreign exchange markets and a $10.4 billion increase in international reserves recorded for August as a whole.

THE ROLE OF THE EURO-DOLLAR MARKET

The Euro-dollar market's contribution to the financing of the 1971 dollar crisis may be examined in terms of two major potential financing roles:

Primary Financing Role

The market's primary financing role, which is based on an allocative or redistributive function, embraces the private withdrawal or securing of deposits to effect speculative or precautionary currency conversions and may be distinguished from an endogenous financing role, based on a generative function, by the exclusion of central banks' depositing newly acquired reserves in the market. This exclusion results in the market's being unable to effect a net increase in dollar claims available for speculative financing, since each Euro-dollar transaction involving the purchase of currencies with withdrawn or borrowed deposits necessitates the transacting of dollar claims held on the US and therefore, irrespective of the primary or endogenously created volume of Euro-dollar deposits in existence, the quantity of Euro-dollars sold to central banks through support operations is necessarily constrained by the quantity of dollar claims already in existence in the US. The Euro-dollar market's primary financing capacity is thus determined by the increased probability that any given level of dollar claims will be used for speculative transactions and by the increased ease with which such transactions may be effected. By attracting dollars which might otherwise have been held in the US as investment, transaction or precautionary balances ("risk-aversive"), the Euro-dollar market is able to convert claims, either directly or indirectly, into speculative ("risk-amenable") balances, and by providing facilities which permit both the rapid securing and withdrawal of deposits (in the latter case call and overnight deposits involve zero liquidation costs), the market is able to effect the expeditious conversion of these balances into stronger currencies.

The market's primary financing role may be examined in terms of four major financing indicators:

US Banks' Liabilities to Foreign Commercial Banks

The withdrawal or securing of Euro-dollar deposits to effect currency conversions and the maintenance of these dollars by central banks in a form other than Euro-dollar deposits will, other things being equal, occasion a net decline in US banks' liabilities to foreign commercial banks corresponding directly to the Euro-dollar deposits originally borrowed or withdrawn. Euro-dollars used for speculative purposes, therefore, will be contained within the general decline in US banks' liabilities to foreign commercial banks which might be expected at times of speculative activity. Examination of changes in these liabilities for the third quarter of 1971 reveals that they declined by $1.9 billion, the greater part of which, however, was accounted for by "other" items, including bankers' acceptances and commercial paper as well as CDs. Deposit liabilities, in contrast, declined by just $10 million. Nor is a clearer financing pattern revealed by monthly changes, for although total liabilities declined by $416 million and $1114 million in July and August respectively -- within which deposit liabilities declined by $605 million and $681 million respectively -- large US banks' deposit liabilities to foreign commercial banks declined by just $36 million in July and actually increased by $48 million in August. Indeed in the few days both immediately preceding and succeeding the suspension of dollar convertibility (in week ending August 18th), deposit liabilities increased by $163 million. On the basis of these changes, therefore, it appears that conventional non-Euro-dollar capital movements accounted for the greater part of changes in US banks' liabilities to foreign commercial banks.

Changes in Reporting Positions

The second financing indicator embraces a comparison of the growth of aggregate market positions with the increase in international exchange reserves recorded in the third quarter of 1971. It might be expected that, if it could be established that the growth of international reserves measured in terms of changes in US liabilities to official foreigners exceeded the increase in aggregate market positions, this would partly indicate the extent to which reserve augmentation was accounted for by sources other than the Euro-dollar market. Whilst this approach serves as an analytically useful point of departure, enabling the August crisis to be placed in a broader Euro-dollar/reserve perspective, it is subject to a number of limitations:

-- Euro-dollar liabilities might be expected to decline during periods of speculative activity as dollars are converted into stronger currencies, in which case a comparison of aggregate Euro-dollar liabilities with reserve increases will serve to understate the volume of speculative flows accounted for by Euro-dollar sources;

-- It is inconceivable that all Euro-dollar credits are extended for speculative purposes and since it is impossible to differentiate between speculative and non-speculative transactions, the inclusion of total Euro-dollar claims in a reserve comparison will serve to overstate the volume of Euro-dollar credits channelled to official reserve agencies;

-- Because of the discrete nature of

aggregate reporting data, it is possible that positions built up and unwound within the relevant accounting period will not be fully reflected in data changes;

-- The existence of deposit pyramiding will inflate total positions and hence distort the volume of final use credit used and potentially usable for speculative financing purposes;

-- The existence of an official Euro-dollar/reserve multiplier will tend to obscure the market's primary financing role;

-- Euro-dollars may be channelled to non-Euro-dollar off-shore centres, thereby distorting speculative flow patterns.

Even taking these limitations into account, a comparison of the respective $0.2 billion and $1.6 billion increases in reporting banks' assets and liabilities (figure 5-1, p. 75) with the $11.3 billion increase in US liquid and non-liquid liabilities to foreign official agencies in the third quarter of 1971 still reveals that (after allowance is made for the exclusion of Swiss trustee funds for which data are not available), official reserves increased by substantially more than Euro-dollar positions. In conjunction with external net switching into non-dollar foreign currencies of just $1 billion in the third quarter of 1971 and a $2 billion increase over the same period in net external domestic currency liabilities which were insufficient to absorb more than a limited proportion of Euro-dollars, it is apparent that a large measure of reserve augmentation was accounted for by sources other than the Euro-dollar market.

Changes in US Banks' Foreign Branch Dollar Positions

A third financing indicator embraces the dollar positions of US banks' foreign branches (table 8). These may be used as a proxy for the component flows contained within aggregate market data and thus afford a sectoral analysis of Euro-dollar flows. Examination of these positions does not reveal an unequivocal financing pattern, however, for whilst the withdrawal of Euro-dollar deposits for speculative financing purposes suggested by the $1.5 billion reduction in reporting banks' total dollar liabilities to non-banks is broadly confirmed by a $245 million decline in foreign branches' liabilities to non-banks in July, this latter decline must be offset

Figure 5-1

XTERNAL DOMESTIC AND FOREIGN CURRENCY POSITIONS OF REPORTING EUROPEAN BA
December 1970 - December 1971

($ billions)

	DOLLARS			OTHER FOREIGN CURRENCIES			DOMESTIC CUR	
	Liabilities	Assets	Net	Liabilities	Assets	Net	Liabilities	Assets
1970	53.8	50.8	- 3.0	15.3	15.7	+ 0.4	13.2	4.7
1971	54.3	51.8	- 2.5	16.4	16.3	- 0.1	13.2	4.9
1971	56.5	55.1	- 1.4	18.6	17.4	- 1.2	13.0	5.7
1971	58.1	55.3	- 2.8	21.4	21.2	- 0.2	14.8	5.5
1971	65.8	61.9	- 3.9	25.7	25.7	---	18.1	5.3
ter	- 1.6	+ 0.2	- 1.4	- 2.8	+ 3.8	+ 1.0	- 1.8	- 0.2

IS Annual Report, 1972

es Swiss positions

against a decrease in liabilities to non-banks of only $22 million reported for the third quarter as a whole. Similarly, liabilities to foreign banks declined by $778 million in July, although against this must again be offset a $1.7 billion increase in August and September and a $2 billion increase in aggregate market liabilities to non-resident banks reported by inside area banks over the third quarter as a whole. Examination of changes in claims also fails to reveal a determinate financing pattern, with declines of $807 million and $41 million on banks and non-banks respectively in July, contrasting with combined increases of $3078 million and $305 million in August and September respectively, whilst aggregate market claims on banks and non-banks declined by $1430 million and $210 million respectively over the third quarter as a whole.

Changes in aggregate market and US banks' foreign branches' positions do not thus exhibit the degree of correspondence which might be expected if the Euro-dollar market had indeed assumed a significant financing role.

Interest Rate Changes

The fourth and final financing indicator is changes in Euro-dollar interest rates which, for the period April 2nd - September 3rd 1971, are illustrated in figure 4-2 (p. 60). Examination of these changes reveals that interest rates remained relatively stable for most of June and July, hardening only in the period immediately preceding the dollar crisis, with call offer rates rising to $6\frac{3}{4}$% by Friday July 30th. Short-term rates continued to fluctuate around this level in the following week, although some further hardening in longer-term rates became apparent. It was not until the second week of August, therefore, that interest rates began to rise significantly, with call and seven-day bid/offer rates increasing by 150 and 138 basis points to 8% and $9\frac{1}{8}$% respectively. This culminated on Friday August 13th in the complete suspension of regular quotations for call and seven-day rates -- a situation which continued throughout the following week until Monday August 23rd when, following the reopening of the exchange markets, call and seven-day deposits were offered at rates of 9% and 10% respectively.

Changes in interest rates thus suggest that pressure developed on both the demand for and supply of Euro-dollar deposits -- with a possible concentration on the supply (bid) side of the market -- and that, whilst this was discernible in the period immediately preceding the crisis, it was not until after the closure of the foreign exchange markets that more intense pressure developed. As had been the case in the Deutsche Mark crisis, therefore, the use of Euro-dollars for speculative financing purposes appears to have been principally concentrated on the period following the suspension of official exchange transactions.

The available evidence thus indicates that changes in interest rates and reporting positions failed to accord with the substantial reserve increases recorded in August and in the third quarter of 1971 as a whole and positively confirms the absence of either the wholesale withdrawal or securing of deposits for speculative financing purposes. The Euro-dollar market's primary financing role in the dollar crisis of 1971 does not seem, therefore, to have assumed significant proportions.

Endogenous Financing Role

The market's endogenous financing role arises from the operation of the official Euro-dollar reserve multiplier which inflates reserves and exacerbates exchange rate pressures through the depositing of official reserves in the Euro-dollar market and the onlending of these deposits to speculators who sell the deposits for currencies which are expected to appreciate. The purchase of these dollars by central banks and the subsequent redepositing of the proceeds in the Euro-dollar market provide the means of financing further rounds of speculation which in turn inflate official reserves and intensify exchange rate pressures. The operation of the official Euro-dollar/reserve multiplier thus requires the successive borrowing, purchasing and official redepositing of Euro-dollars in the market.

International reserve inflation and the intensification of exchange rate pressures may also result from the speculative activities of central banks themselves whose role may be considered within the present context, directly involving, as it does, the Euro-dollar market. The significance of the role of central banks derives from the fact that speculation may be financed without there being a readily discernible financing pattern. If a central bank diversifies its dollar claims on the US by purchasing, for example, Deutsche Marks from the Bundesbank, there will be an identifiable decline in US liabilities to the central bank selling the dollars and an increase in liabilities to the Bundesbank (assuming that the latter maintains its reserves in the US). Similarly, if a non-official institution either withdraws Euro-dollars from the market or else draws on claims held in the US to finance Deutsche Mark purchases and if the Bundesbank maintains the proceeds either in the Euro-dollar market or in the US, there will be a discernible financing pattern involving a decline in private Euro-dollar/US claims and an increase in official Euro-dollar/US claims. If, however, central banks withdraw Euro-dollars for speculative financing purposes and the dollar receipts are redeposited in the Euro-dollar market, this will result in a zero change in Euro-dollar positions (this may be contrasted with the increase in both Euro-dollar assets and liabilities resulting from the operation of the official Euro-dollar/reserve multiplier), downward pressure on the dollar, and an increase in official reserves which will be identifiable only as an increase in the international exchange reserve residual.

This process of reserve augmentation is illustrated in figure 5-2 (p. 79), in which "Euro-banks" represent the Euro-dollar market, central bank A represents the Bank of England, central bank B the Bundesbank and domestic bank B a German commercial bank. For ease of exposition, an exchange rate of $1 = £1 = DM 1 is assumed. The process commences when central bank A withdraws its $10 deposit from the Euro-dollar market and proceeds to purchase DM 10 which, because of speculative pressure on the Deutsche Mark, are supplied by central bank B. Central bank A will now hold a Deutsche Mark claim on domestic bank B (the contra entry to which will be an increase in domestic reserves held with central bank B), whilst central bank B in turn will hold a dollar claim on the US. If this latter claim is subsequently transferred to the Euro-

Figure 5-2

RESERVE CREATION AND THE WITHDRAWAL OF OFFICIAL EURO-DOLLAR RESERVES

(Exchange rate: $1 = £1 = DM 1)

EURO-BANKS

LIABILITIES $		ASSETS $	
Position 1			
Time deposit Central Bank A	10	Demand deposit with US Bank	10
Position 2			
Time deposit Central Bank A	-10	Demand deposit with US Bank	10
Time deposit Central Bank B	+10		
NET CHANGE	0		0
Final Position			
Time deposit Central Bank B	10	Demand deposit with US Bank	10

CENTRAL BANK A

LIABILITIES £		ASSETS (RESERVES) $	
Position 1			
Various	10	Time deposit with Euro-banks	10
Position 2			
Various	10	Time deposit with Euro-banks	-10
		Time deposit with Domestic Bank B	+10
NET CHANGE	0		0
Final Position			
Various	10	Time deposit with Domestic Bank B	10

CENTRAL BANK B

LIABILITIES DM		ASSETS (RESERVES) $	
Final Position			
Domestic Bank B	+10	Time deposit with Euro-banks	+10
NET CHANGE	+10		+10

DOMESTIC BANK B

LIABILITIES DM		ASSETS DM	
Final Position			
Time deposit Central Bank A	+10	Demand deposit with Central Bank B	+10
NET CHANGE	+10		+10

EXCHANGE RESERVE RESIDUAL

Position 1	Central Bank A	10
Position 2	Central Bank A	10
	Central Bank B	+10

TOTAL NET CHANGES

	Liabilities		Assets
Euro-banks	---		---
Central Bank A	---		---
Central Bank B	+10		+10
Domestic Bank B	+10		+10
Exchange Reserve Residual		+10	

dollar market, the result will be (final positions in figure 5-2): a zero net change in Euro-dollar positions; a zero net change in central bank A's exchange reserves; a $10 increase in the reserves of central bank B (equivalent to the $10 increase in the exchange reserve residual); and a DM 10 increase in the external liabilities of domestic bank B. More significantly, the dollar will have been subjected to selling pressure without this pressure being readily identifiable in the form of financing flows, since the only discernible financing indicator will have been an increase in the international exchange reserve residual.

An assessment of the impact of these flows as well as of the Euro-dollar market's "pure" endogenous financing role, in the absence of specific data, must rely upon more generalised measures: US liquid and non-liquid liabilities to official institutions increased by $2.3 billion and $7.6 billion in July and August respectively, within which increases were reported for all major geographical areas. This would indicate the absence of any significant sectoral decline in official dollar claims on the US during the dollar crisis. Changes in US banks' foreign branches' liabilities to official institutions, however, reveal a different financing pattern, for they do not record an increase in official Euro-dollar deposits -- as might have been expected if the official Euro-dollar/reserve multiplier had exerted a significant financing impact -- nor a zero net change in deposits -- if official deposits had been withdrawn and subsequently redeposited in the Euro-dollar market by the recipient central bank -- but rather a decline in deposits corresponding to an increase in official non-dollar-denominated holdings of Euro-currencies. Thus in July and August 1971 official dollar claims on US banks' foreign branches declined by $188 million and $41 million respectively whilst non-dollar claims increased by $222 million and $118 million respectively. Corresponding to these changes, the international exchange reserve residual increased by $1.9 billion in the third quarter of 1971.

These changes suggest that central banks did not remain aloof from exploiting the opportunities afforded by prospective exchange realignments and that, consequently, official reserve movements were compatible with capital flows of a destabilising nature. They do not, however, support the existence of significant endogenous Euro-dollar financing.

Changes in US Payments Data

Evaluation of the Euro-dollar market's speculative financing role would be incomplete without an examination of alternative speculative financing sources, most important of which are US capital outflows.

-- Receipts of income on US direct investments abroad, having been on a rising trend in the sixties, increasing from $2.4 billion in 1960 to $5 billion in 1970, and having reached an historic quarterly peak of $1.5 billion in the second quarter of 1971, subsequently declined to $1.1 billion in the following quarter, thereafter rising to $2.1 billion in the final quarter, suggesting that repatriations may have been delayed to benefit from anticipated exchange realignments.

-- Payments of income on direct foreign investments in the US also exhibited a rising trend in the sixties, but changes in 1971 do not support the existence of an acceleration of repatriations in the third quarter of that year.

-- US direct investments abroad failed to exhibit any untoward changes in the third quarter of 1971.

-- Foreign direct investment in the US recorded quarterly inflows throughout most of the sixties and the early part of the seventies but recorded a marked outflow of $437 million in the third quarter of 1971, suggesting the postponement of foreign direct investment in advance of an imminent exchange rate realignment.

-- US holdings of foreign securities failed to exhibit any untoward increase in the third quarter of 1971, increasing by $346 million compared to the $408 million and $368 million increases recorded in the first two quarters of the year.

-- Foreign holdings of US corporate securities increased by $626 million in the third quarter of 1971 and consequently failed to reflect a significant liquidation of dollar investments for speculative purposes.

-- Foreign private holdings of US Treasury bonds and notes exhibited a marginal decline

($58 million) in the third quarter of 1971 which, although concentrated on August ($36 million) was nevertheless too small to be of major financing significance.

-- Long-term private claims reported by US non-banks increased by a negligible $37 million in the third quarter of 1971 whilst bank reported claims, which had declined throughout the latter half of the sixties, increased by $153 million and $247 million in the second and third quarters of the year respectively.

-- Long-term private liabilities reported by US banks declined by $71 million in the third quarter of 1971 whilst non-bank reported liabilities, which had increased throughout most of the sixties, declined by $191 million in the third quarter of the year.

-- US banks' liabilities to international and regional organisations increased by $137 million in the third quarter of 1971 whilst liabilities to non-banks declined by $312 million, although the impact of this decline was mitigated by the fact that only $55 million occurred in August (liabilities to banks were considered in terms of the Euro-dollar market's primary financing role, pp. 72 - 73).

-- Short-term claims on foreigners reported by US banks increased by $822 million in the third quarter of 1971, $341 million of which represented short-term liquid claims and $90 million claims denominated in foreign currencies. Since only $94 million was accounted for by claims on official institutions, collections outstanding and acceptances made for the account of foreigners, and since total claims increased by $1.5 billion in August (declines of $0.1 billion and $0.6 billion being recorded in July and September respectively), increases in US banks' short-term claims on foreigners appear to have constituted a potentially important source of speculative financing.

-- The penultimate source of dollar financing consists of increases in US non-banks' short-term liquid claims on foreigners, which increased by $143 million in the third quarter of 1971. Within this total, foreign currency claims reported by large non-banking concerns increased by $30 million, whilst in August total dollar and non-dollar claims increased by $148 million and $35 million respectively. Although these increases were not substantial, they were potentially significant, for they confirmed the existence of dollar outflows and increases in US non-dollar claims which, in conjunction with the substantial increase in errors and omissions, may be expected to have made a significant contribution to speculative financing.

-- The final and potentially most significant source of financing is the US net errors and omissions item which, having accelerated to $2.3 billion in the second quarter of 1971 (a period also characterised by currency instability), then surged to a record $4.6 billion ($5.1 billion seasonally adjusted) in the third quarter of the year -- a level which only began to be approached again in the dollar crisis of 1973. Since a dollar outflow of such exceptional magnitude may clearly be expected to have been influenced by speculative and hedging considerations, it appears that the $4.6 billion increase in errors and omissions recorded in the third quarter of 1971 constituted a significant source of speculative financing.

Evidence relating to Euro-dollar and US capital flows thus reveals a speculative financing pattern which serves to incriminate the Euro-dollar market less than might at first have been expected. It is clear that the Euro-dollar market contributed to the financing of the August dollar crisis, but changes in interest rates and reporting positions indicate that the market's primary financing role was limited and did not constitute the principal source of speculative activity. Certainly there is no evidence to support the wholesale withdrawal, securing or switching of Euro-dollar deposits for speculative financing purposes; nor is there evidence to support a significant endogenous financing role, although changes in reporting positions suggest that an element of official Euro-dollar reserve diversification may have attended the currency crisis. US capital outflows, in contrast, assumed significant proportions and might consequently be expected to have made a substantial contribution to speculative activity. It may be concluded, therefore, that the principal source of speculative financing in the 1971 dollar crisis was US capital outflows effected through conventional rather than specific Euro-dollar channels.

Chapter Six

THE 1973 DOLLAR CRISIS

The 1973 dollar crisis was significant not only because it occurred just twelve months after the Smithsonian Agreement purported to have effected a fundamental realignment of international exchange rates, but also because it represented the disintegration of the remaining vestiges of Bretton Woods. It constituted, moreover, a development of major international consequence in which the Euro-dollar market assumed a significant financing role.

The crisis began in early 1973 with the announcement, on January 22nd, of the establishment of a dual exchange market in which the commercial lira would be maintained within fixed margins and the financial lira would be free to float. This announcement did little, however, to deter lira outflows which, together with a continuing high level of dollar sales, brought the Swiss franc to its upper intervention point against the dollar. On January 23rd, following heavy and sustained support measures, the Swiss authorities withdrew from the market and the Swiss franc was allowed to float. These developments were interpreted as reflecting increased willingness to resort to exchange rate flexibility to counter unwanted capital inflows, and consequently subjected the dollar to further pressure which assumed crisis proportions following the disclosure of an increase in the US current account deficit for 1972 to $9.7 billion. Between Thursday February 1st and the official closure of the foreign exchange markets on Friday February 9th, the Group of Ten purchased approximately $8 billion - $10 billion in support operations, with Germany accounting for approximately $6 billion. Dollar purchases on Friday alone amounted to $2 billion, with Germany's share amounting to approximately $1.7 billion.

In contrast to the delay which had characterised the 1971 crisis, the announcement on Monday February 12th that the US President would request Congress to authorise a 10% devaluation of the dollar represented a concerted attempt to effect a rapid solution to the crisis. This attempt proved of limited success, however, for the dollar began to weaken again from Wednesday February 21st onwards and, following the purchase of $2.7 billion by the Bundesbank on Thursday March 1st, the foreign exchange markets were closed. When the markets were eventually reopened on Monday March 19th, the major trading currencies were floating against the dollar. The era of floating exchange rates had arrived.

THE FINANCING ROLE OF THE EURO-DOLLAR MARKET

The Euro-dollar market's contribution to the financing of the 1973 dollar crisis may again be examined in terms of two major financing roles:

Primary Financing Role

Interest Rate Changes

The basic financing pattern to emerge from changes in interest rates (figure 6-1, p. 86) is that pressure on the dollar corresponded, in varying degrees, to pressure on both Euro-dollar and Euro-Deutsche Mark interest rates. The first wave of speculative dollar pressure developed on Thursday February 1st and although this was not immediately manifested in changes in Euro-dollar rates, there was a steady decline in Euro-Deutsche Mark rates as dollars, converted into Deutsche Marks, were deposited in the Euro-Deutsche Mark market in an attempt to avoid the restrictions imposed on on-shore Deutsche Mark deposits. As pressure intensified, Euro-dollar rates hardened and on Tuesday February 6th the regular quotation of call deposits was suspended, whilst seven-day bid and offer rates increased by 38 basis points. Pressure continued to develop and on Friday February 9th, corresponding to the closure of the exchange markets and the Bundesbank's purchasing an estimated $1.7 billion

Figure 6-1

EURO-DOLLAR AND EURO-DEUTSCHE MARK BID AND OFFER RATES

January 26th - March 30th 1973

(% p.a.)

	EURO-D. MARKS	EURO-DOLLARS			
	Short-term[1]	Call	7 Days	1 Month	3 Months
h Jan	$3\frac{1}{2}$ - 4	$5\frac{3}{4}$ - $6\frac{1}{4}$	6 - $6\frac{1}{2}$	$6\frac{1}{8}$ - $6\frac{5}{8}$	$6\frac{1}{4}$ - 6
h Jan	4 - $4\frac{1}{2}$	$5\frac{7}{8}$ - $6\frac{3}{8}$	6 - $6\frac{1}{2}$	$6\frac{1}{8}$ - $6\frac{5}{8}$	$6\frac{1}{4}$ - 6
h Jan	$5\frac{3}{4}$ - $6\frac{1}{2}$	$5\frac{7}{8}$ - $6\frac{5}{8}$	6 - $6\frac{5}{8}$	$6\frac{3}{8}$ - $6\frac{7}{8}$	$6\frac{1}{2}$ - 7
t Jan	4 - $4\frac{1}{2}$	$5\frac{7}{8}$ - $6\frac{3}{8}$	6 - $6\frac{1}{2}$	$6\frac{3}{8}$ - $6\frac{7}{8}$	$6\frac{3}{8}$ - 6
t Feb	$1\frac{3}{4}$ - $2\frac{1}{4}$	$5\frac{3}{4}$ - $6\frac{1}{4}$	$5\frac{7}{8}$ - $6\frac{3}{8}$	$6\frac{3}{8}$ - $6\frac{7}{8}$	$6\frac{1}{2}$ - 7
d Feb	$\frac{1}{4}$ - $\frac{5}{8}$	$5\frac{7}{8}$ - $6\frac{3}{8}$	$6\frac{1}{8}$ - $6\frac{5}{8}$	$6\frac{5}{8}$ - $7\frac{1}{8}$	$6\frac{5}{8}$ - 7
h Feb	0 - $\frac{1}{4}$	$5\frac{7}{8}$ - $6\frac{3}{8}$	$6\frac{1}{8}$ - $6\frac{5}{8}$	$6\frac{1}{2}$ - 7	$6\frac{3}{4}$ - 7
h Feb	(- $\frac{1}{4}$)- $\frac{1}{4}$	---	$6\frac{1}{2}$ - 7	$6\frac{11}{16}$ - $7\frac{3}{16}$	$6\frac{13}{16}$ - 7
h Feb	0 - (- 1)	---	$6\frac{1}{2}$ - 7	$6\frac{1}{2}$ - 7	$6\frac{9}{16}$ - 7
h Feb	0 - (- 1)	$6\frac{3}{8}$ - $6\frac{7}{8}$	$6\frac{5}{8}$ - $7\frac{1}{8}$	$6\frac{3}{4}$ - $7\frac{1}{4}$	$6\frac{7}{8}$ - 7
h Feb	(-25)- (-15)	---	---	$7\frac{3}{8}$ - $7\frac{7}{8}$	$7\frac{1}{4}$ - 7
h Feb	---	---	$12\frac{1}{2}$ - $14\frac{1}{2}$	$8\frac{1}{2}$ - $9\frac{1}{8}$	$7\frac{1}{2}$ - 8
h Feb	(- 4)- (- 2)	---	8 - $8\frac{1}{2}$	7 - $7\frac{1}{2}$	$6\frac{7}{8}$ - 7

eb	(- 8)- (- 3)	---	7 5/8 - 7 3/4	6 7/8 - 7 3/8	6 3/4 - 7 1/4	
eb	(-10)- (- 5)	---	8 7/8 - 9 1/8	7 3/4 - 7 7/8	7 1/8 - 7 5/8	
eb	(-15)- (- 5)	---	8 3/4 - 9 1/4	7 5/8 - 8 1/8	7 1/4 - 7 3/4	
eb	(-12)- (-11)	---	8 7/8 - 9 3/8	7 7/8 - 8 3/8	7 3/8 - 7 7/8	
eb	(-10)- (- 8)	---	---	8 1/8 - 8 5/8	7 3/4 - 8 1/4	
eb	(- 5)- 0	---	---	8 3/16 - 8 9/16	7 9/16 - 8 1/16	
eb	(- 2)- 0	---	---	7 7/8 - 8 7/8	7 7/8 - 8 7/8	
eb	(- 5)- 0	---	11 1/2 - 12 1/2	8 7/8 - 9 7/8	8 - 8 1/2	R
eb	(- 5)- 0	---	11 - 12	8 7/8 - 9 3/8	8 1/4 - 8 3/4	s
eb	(- 4)- (- 1)	*	8 1/4 - 9 1/4	8 3/8 - 8 7/8	8 - 8 1/2	p
eb	(- 2 1/2)- (-1 1/2)	*	8 1/2 - 9 1/2	8 1/2 - 9	8 1/4 - 8 3/4	t
ar	(-25)- (-15)	*	11 - 15	10 - 10 1/2	9 1/4 - 9 3/4	
ar	(-25)- (-15)	---	10 - 12	9 3/4 - 10 1/4	8 5/8 - 9 1/8	
ar	(-10)- (- 5)	---	9 - 10	9 1/8 - 9 5/8	8 3/8 - 8 7/8	
ar	(- 6)- (- 4)	8 3/4 - 9 1/4	9 - 9 1/2	8 7/8 - 9 3/8	8 1/4 - 8 3/4	
ar	(- 3)- 0	8 3/4 - 9 1/4	9 1/8 - 9 5/8	8 7/8 - 9 3/8	8 3/8 - 8 7/8	E
ar	(- 4)- 0	9 - 9 1/2	9 1/8 - 9 3/8	9 3/8 - 9 7/8	8 1/2 - 9	m
ar	(- 4)- (- 1)	---	9 1/8 - 9 5/8	9 5/8 - 10 1/8	8 5/8 - 9 1/8	c
ar	(- 3)- (- 1)	7 3/8 - 8 1/4	7 1/2 - 9 1/4	8 1/8 - 8 5/8	8 1/8 - 8 5/8	
ar	(- 5)- (- 3)	7 1/4 - 7 3/4	7 1/2 - 8	7 3/4 - 8 1/4	7 3/4 - 8 1/4	

Figure 6-1 (cont'd)

	EURO-D. MARKS	EURO-DOLLARS			
	Short-term[1]	Call	7 Days	1 Month	3 Month
Mar	(- 6)- (- 4)	$7\frac{5}{8}$ - $8\frac{1}{8}$	$7\frac{5}{8}$ - $8\frac{1}{8}$	$7\frac{3}{4}$ - $8\frac{1}{4}$	$7\frac{3}{4}$ - 8
Mar	(-15)- (-10)	---	$7\frac{5}{8}$ - $8\frac{1}{8}$	$8\frac{1}{16}$ - $8\frac{9}{16}$	$7\frac{15}{16}$ - 8
Mar	(-15)- (-10)	$7\frac{5}{8}$ - $8\frac{1}{8}$	$7\frac{3}{4}$ - $8\frac{1}{4}$	8 - $8\frac{1}{2}$	8 - 8
Mar	(-15)- (-11)	$7\frac{1}{4}$ - $7\frac{3}{4}$	$7\frac{1}{2}$ - 8	8 - $8\frac{1}{2}$	8 - 8
Mar	(- 3)- 0	---	---	$8\frac{3}{4}$ - $9\frac{1}{4}$	$8\frac{7}{16}$ - 8
Mar	(- 1)- (- $\frac{1}{2}$)	$7\frac{3}{4}$ - $8\frac{1}{4}$	$7\frac{7}{8}$ - $8\frac{1}{8}$	$8\frac{1}{8}$ - $8\frac{5}{8}$	$8\frac{3}{8}$ - 8

nal offer rates 25% - 55%

Financial Times, various issues

days' notice

in support operations, pressure on Euro-dollar and Euro-Deutsche Mark rates became such that regular quotations for both call and seven-day Euro-dollar deposits were suspended whilst short-term Euro-Deutsche Mark deposits were quoted at negative bid and offer rates of -25% and -15% respectively. Following the closure of the exchange markets on Friday 9th, a pattern of interest rate changes similar to that identified in the two 1971 crises emerged, with the prospect of a second dollar devaluation engendering both withdrawals of, and demands for Euro-dollar deposits. By the close of business on Monday February 12th, average Euro-dollar bid/offer rates for seven-day deposits had almost doubled to 13½% from their previous level of 6⅞% on Thursday 8th.

When the markets eventually reopened on Wednesday February 14th, increased supplies of Deutsche Marks and the substantial premium on forward Deutsche Marks occasioned further reductions in Euro-Deutsche Mark rates which declined to bid levels of -15%, whilst regular Euro-dollar call rates remained generally unobtainable. An indication of the underlying pressure was provided by the suspension, between Tuesday 20th and Thursday 22nd, of regular Euro-dollar rates for seven-day deposits which, following the restoration of quotes on Friday 23rd, attracted bid and offer rates of 11½% and 12½% respectively. In the following week pressure intensified and when the exchange markets were eventually closed at the end of business on Thursday March 1st -- after the Bundesbank had purchased an estimated $2.7 billion -- Euro-dollar call deposits were being quoted at nominal rates of between 25% and 55%, seven-day deposits at bid and offer rates of 11% and 15% respectively and short-term Euro-Deutsche Mark bid and offer rates at negative levels of -25% and -15% respectively.

The evidence relating to changes in interest rates thus indicates that, in marked contrast to the Deutsche Mark and dollar crises of 1971 in which Euro-dollar demand essentially developed after foreign exchange markets had been closed, Euro-dollar deposits were actually subjected to considerable financing pressure during the course of the 1973 dollar crisis.

Changes in Reporting Positions

Changes in reporting banks' foreign currency positions vis-à-vis bank and non-bank non-residents (tables 7(i)-7(iii)) reveal that non-bank dollar and non-dollar positions remained remarkably stable in the first quarter of 1973. Dollar claims on, and liabilities to non-banks increased by $1110 million and $1130 million respectively, whilst non-dollar claims on, and liabilities to non-banks increased by $1230 million and $1120 million respectively, with the result that changes in net dollar and non-dollar positions amounted to a negligible $20 million and $1110 million respectively. The limited size of these positions is somewhat surprising and, although the changes must be qualified since data exclude Swiss trustee funds, both the direction and general magnitude of these changes are confirmed not only by US banks' foreign branch positions vis-à-vis non-banks-- which increased in January and February by net liabilities of just $76 million and $93 million respectively and in March by net assets of $118 million (table 8), -- but also by German banks' gross external liabilities to non-banks which increased in February and March by a negligible $97 million and $48 million respectively. Euro-dollar activity was thus principally accounted for by changes in positions vis-à-vis banks and it may be seen from tables 7(i) and 7(ii) that reporting banks' claims on, and liabilities to other banks decreased by $1 billion and increased by $4.2 billion respectively, resulting in a $5.3 billion increase in net liabilities in the first quarter of 1973 (figure 6-2, p. 91). Since banks' net dollar claims on residents increased by a modest $0.7 billion over the same period, this indicates that reporting banks converted approximately $4.6 billion out of dollars on external account in the first quarter of 1973, a figure which was more than sufficient to account for the $2.2 billion increase in banks' net external liabilities in domestic currencies. Indeed, since reporting banks' net external Deutsche Mark claims increased by $4.3 billion whilst German banks' net external domestic currency liabilities (principally vis-à-vis banks) increased by $1.2 billion (gross liabilities increased by $2.5 billion), it appears that a significant volume of Euro-dollars was identifiably converted into Deutsche Marks in the first quarter of 1973.

Figure 6-2

XTERNAL DOMESTIC AND FOREIGN CURRENCY POSITIONS OF REPORTING EUROPEAN BAN

December 1972 - March 1973

($ billions)

		December 1972	March 1973
	Liabilities	96.7	102.1
	Assets	98.0	98.1
	Net	+ 1.3	- 4.0
	Liabilities	35.2	41.9
OREIGN CURRENCIES	Assets	33.8	43.1
	Net	- 1.4	+ 1.2
	Liabilities	25.0	29.3
C CURRENCY	Assets	13.0	15.1
	Net	- 12.0	- 14.2

S Annual Report, 1974

s Swiss trustee funds

Changes in US Banks' Foreign Branch Dollar Positions

The net dollar liabilities of US banks' foreign branches increased by $1.4 billion in the first quarter of 1973, $1 billion of which was recorded in February alone (table 8). This may be contrasted with the modest net changes recorded in previous years, including the crisis period of August 1971. Perhaps even more striking, however, were the changes reported in liabilities to, and claims on the US. These increased and decreased by $471 million and $607 million respectively and corresponded to a substantial $2 billion first quarter increase in reporting banks' aggregate liabilities to the US. These flows indicate that US banks made a substantial volume of dollars available at a time of mounting pressure on the dollar and hence that the $1 billion movement out of dollars reported by US banks' foreign branches in February 1973 may be expected to have made a significant contribution to the financing of the 1973 dollar crisis.

The evidence relating to changes in interest rates, aggregate reporting positions and the dollar positions of US banks' foreign branches thus indicates a high degree of correspondence amongst all three principal financing indicators. Increases in Euro-dollar rates together with the absence of wholesale deposit withdrawals suggest that financing pressure was principally concentrated on the credit side of the market, whilst the marked swing in aggregate reporting positions from net assets of $1.3 billion in the fourth quarter of 1972 to net liabilities of $4 billion in the first quarter of 1973 indicates that banks were responsible for effecting a substantial movement out of dollars. It may be concluded, therefore, that, in contrast to previous currency crises in which the Euro-dollar market had assumed a limited financing role, the Euro-dollar market's primary financing role made an important contribution both to the financing of the 1973 dollar crisis and to the intensification of exchange rate pressures.

Endogenous Financing Role

Evaluation of the market's endogenous financing role is complicated by the extended nature of the 1973 crisis and by the inconclusive pattern of identifiable capital flows. US banks' foreign branch liabilities to official institutions increased by a significant $767 million in January but in the following period, when currency instability might have been expected to occasion similar or larger increases, liabilities to official institutions increased by only $128 million and actually decreased by $37 million in February and March respectively.

The inconclusive pattern of these flows was compounded, moreover, by the effective sterilisation in the US of $5.5 billion of the $5.7 billion increase in German dollar reserves reported in February. This served to further reduce the volume of dollar reserves available for endogenous Euro-dollar financing.

Whilst these flows do not necessarily preclude the existence of non-dollar forms of official Euro-currency holdings (external Deutsche Mark liabilities reported by the Bundesbank increased by $1.3 billion in the first quarter of 1973), they nevertheless suggest that the Euro-dollar market's endogenous financing role was limited in both scope and impact and consequently did not make a significant contribution to the financing of the 1973 dollar crisis nor to the intensification of exchange rate pressures.

Changes in US Payments Data

The majority of US capital outflows exhibited modest or negligible increases in the first quarter of 1973. This was more than offset, however, by a small number of very substantial capital outflows. Neither receipts of income on US direct investments abroad nor payments of income on direct foreign investments in the US reflected any untoward changes, declining only marginally from $2.3 billion to $2 billion and from $212 million to $144 million respectively during the first quarter of 1973. Similar marginal declines were recorded in US holdings of foreign securities ($30 million) and foreign private holdings of US corporate securities and US Treasury bonds and notes ($51 million and $49 million). Long-term private liabilities reported by US banks and non-banks increased by $153 million and $255 million respectively. In contrast to the constrained pattern of these capital movements, however, direct investment flows and long-term foreign claims exhibited more pronounced changes: foreign direct investment in the US increased by $371 million in the first quarter of 1973 compared to a decline of $437 million in the third quarter of 1971 which had potentially reflected investment "lagging" in response to prospective exchange realignments, but this increase was more than offset by an increase in US direct investment abroad which dramatically accelerated from $306 million in the final quarter of 1972 to $2.5 billion in the first quarter of 1973. Long-term private foreign claims reported by US banks and non-banks increased by $416 million in the first quarter of 1973, although this represented a slight deceleration from the previous quarter's increase of $537 million. US banks' liabilities to non-banks and international and regional organisations exhibited negligible changes in the first quarter of 1973. Liabilities to foreign commercial banks, in contrast, declined by $1.9 billion over the same period, with a $2 billion decline occurring in February alone. These declines were consistent with the $1 billion decrease in reporting banks' aggregate dollar claims on banks recorded in the first quarter of 1973 (table 7(ii)) and, whilst these declines cannot be interpreted as definitive proof of a Euro-dollar financing role, they nevertheless indicate that foreign commercial banks effected substantial reductions in dollar claims on the US banking system at a time of severe currency instability. Substantial changes were also recorded in US banks' short-term claims on foreigners, which increased by $2.7 billion in the first quarter of 1973, of which short-term liquid claims accounted for $1.2 billion. The greatest increase ($2 billion) was concentrated on February, suggesting that US banks were again instrumental in placing a substantial volume of dollar resources at the disposal of US non-residents at a time of currency instability. The penultimate source of dollar financing was US non-banks' short-term liquid claims which increased by an historic $811 million in the first quarter of 1973, $531 million of which was recorded in February. These claims, considered in conjunction with errors and omissions, suggest that non-banks constituted a potentially important source of dollar financing. The final source of financing was errors and omissions, which increased by

$3.5 billion in the first quarter of 1973. This corresponded closely with increases recorded in the second and third quarters of 1971 and suggests, once again, that conventional US, rather than specific Euro-dollar capital outflows were the principal source of speculative dollar financing.

A synthesis of changes in Euro-dollar positions and US outflows thus indicates that the Euro-dollar market made a non-marginal contribution to the financing of the 1973 dollar crisis. Whilst there is insufficient evidence of an unequivocal nature to identify a significant endogenous financing role, the principal financing indicators relating to changes in interest rates, aggregate reporting positions and US banks' foreign branch positions all point towards substantial Euro-dollar movements which were consistent with a primary financing role. This is not to attribute responsibility for the crisis solely to the Euro-dollar market, however, nor to deny the existence of alternative financing sources, for the acceleration in US direct investment abroad and increases in errors and omissions and short-term claims reported by banks constituted a prodigious source of "conventional" dollar financing which would have been sufficient to account for a substantial portion of the increase in international reserves recorded in the first quarter of 1973 -- a fact explicitly recognised by the Bundesbank:

> The popular slogan according to which the European currencies have been overrun by the 'vagabond dollars' of the Euro-market hardly stands up to an accurate analysis. Particularly during the monetary crisis in February and March 1973, the main portion of the dollars accruing to other countries most likely emanated from the United States itself, although the Euro-banks may well have exercised a turn-table function and facilitated financing... Obviously, the financing of these various transfers of funds [inflows into Germany] is in large measure independent of Euro-dollar credits. Only in the final stage of the exchange

crises in February and March 1973 would purely speculative transactions involving borrowing on the Euro-dollar market seem to have played a major part.[1]

THE MARKET AND CAPITAL CONTROLS

The early seventies, in contrast to the late sixties, were characterised by capital controls specifically designed to curb unwanted inflows rather than outflows of capital. The major controls and the principal countries affected between the latter half of 1971 and 1973 were:

Belgium/Luxembourg

-- Marginal reserve requirements on external convertible franc accounts were progressively increased to 100% by April 1973.

-- With effect from April 1st 1973, a negative interest rate of 0.25% per week was imposed on holdings of convertible franc accounts in excess of daily average holdings in the last quarter of 1972.

-- Non-resident acquisitions of domestic assets continued to be channelled through the free, as opposed to the official franc market.

France

-- With effect from August 21st 1971, a dual exchange market was established and the financial franc market was subsequently merged with the security currency market.

-- With effect from March 21st 1973, a 100% reserve requirement was imposed on increases after January 4th 1973 in non-residents' demand and time deposits denominated in francs. Such increases were subsequently subjected to a negative interest rate of 0.75% per month.

Germany

-- On March 1st 1972, the celebrated cash-deposit scheme (Bardepot) was introduced whereby residents, including banks, were required to lodge non-interest-bearing cash deposits with the Bundesbank, corresponding to 40%

of loans and credits secured either directly or indirectly from non-residents. The first DM 2 million of any such credit was exempted from the scheme. On July 1st 1972, the ratio was raised to 50% and the exemption lowered to DM 500,000, a level which was subsequently reduced to DM 50,000 on January 1st 1973.

-- With effect from July 1st 1972, reserve requirements of 100% were imposed on selected external liabilities.

-- Restrictions continued to apply to non-residents' purchases of domestic assets.

The Netherlands

-- The "O-guilder" circuit was established on September 6th 1971, through which non-residents' purchases and sales of guilder bonds had to be channelled.

-- External borrowing by residents was severely curtailed from July 17th 1972.

-- With effect from March 26th 1973, a negative interest rate of 0.25% per week was imposed on increases in convertible guilder deposits above the levels outstanding in February 1973.

Italy

The general weakness of the lira orientated controls towards the restriction of outflows, rather than inflows of capital, and resulted in the establishment of a dual exchange market on January 22nd 1973.

Switzerland

-- With effect from August 16th 1971, marginal reserve requirements of 100% were imposed on increases in net external deposit liabilities. Although these requirements were subsequently varied, they were generally maintained at high levels.

-- Increases in non-residents' investment in real estate were frozen in June 1972.

-- With effect from July 3rd 1972, a negative interest rate of 2% per quarter was imposed on increases in external franc deposits reported after June 30th 1972.

Japan

The dominant feature of Japanese capital controls was the liberalisation of existing regulations restricting capital outflows. Additional measures included:

-- With effect from June 1st 1972, marginal reserve requirements of 25% were imposed on increases in non-resident free Yen accounts. These requirements were subsequently raised to 50% in the following July.

-- With effect from October 21st 1972, restrictions were imposed on non-resident purchases of domestic securities.

The UK

Although measures designed to restrict capital inflows were introduced in the period August 1971 to June 1972, they were essentially of minor importance and, following the floating of sterling, were mostly abandoned.

The US

The US was characterised by an absence of measures specifically designed to curb capital outflows. Those measures which were introduced subsequent to the dollar crisis, however, essentially restored equality to the terms under which US banks could compete for domestic and Euro-dollar funds:

-- With effect from May 16th 1973, Regulation Q ceilings were suspended on single maturity time deposits of $100,000 and over with maturities of ninety days or more (ceilings on equivalent deposits with maturities of less than ninety days had been suspended on June 24th 1970).[2]

-- With effect from June 21st 1973, marginal reserve requirements on time deposits of $100,000 or more were raised to 8% while the 20% reserve requirement on US banks' Euro-dollar borrowings and foreign branch loans to US residents was reduced to 8%.

The extensive network of capital controls assembled in the early seventies failed to prevent a second dollar devaluation and, given the significance of the Euro-dollar market as a financing source, it may be asked whether the market had indeed become so powerful that it was unilaterally able to breach these controls. An affirmative answer would not, however, seem appropriate since:

Firstly, negative interest rates of 2% per quarter were insufficient to deter speculative inflows in the light of substantial anticipated exchange realignments;

Secondly, high marginal reserve requirements may be expected to curb only the domestic multiplicative impact of capital inflows and hence would be of limited success in alleviating the exchange rate pressures resulting from initial capital inflows;

Thirdly, dual exchange markets are only temporary palliatives and are consequently incapable of effecting permanent corrections to exchange rate imbalances;

Fourthly, with specific reference to the German Bardepot scheme, cash-deposit ratios were often insufficient to offset the cost advantages of external borrowing. When the scheme was first introduced in March 1972 with a cash-deposit ratio of 40%, the ratio was already barely sufficient to absorb the cost differential in favour of Euro-Deutsche Mark borrowing (figure 6-3, p. 100), and the subsequent dramatic decline in Euro-Deutsche Mark rates to levels as low as 2% p.a. for prime commercial borrowers in the third quarter of 1972 consequently further widened differentials in favour of Euro-Deutsche Marks, despite the raising of the cash-deposit ratio to 50% on July 1st. Certainly the reduction in the cash-deposit exemption from DM 500,000 to DM 50,000 could hardly be expected to have acted as a serious deterrent to external borrowing when domestic Deutsche Mark prime rates soared to over 8% and Euro-Deutsche Mark prime rates plummeted to levels as low as 1% in the first quarter of 1973. Even if the scheme had been applied more flexibly, moreover, it is unlikely that it would have exerted other than a marginally ameliorative impact, since the DM 2.8 billion increase in German corporate external short-term Deutsche Mark liabilities in July and August occasioned by a substantial borrowing differential in favour of Euro-Deutsche Marks accounted for only a small proportion of the increase in total German reserves and occurred in different forms and at different times to the speculative inflows of 1973.

Figure 6-3

DOMESTIC DEUTSCHE MARK PRIME LENDING RATES AND EURO-DEUTSCHE MARK PRIME LENDING RATES WITH CASH DEPOSIT RATIOS
January 1972 - March 1973

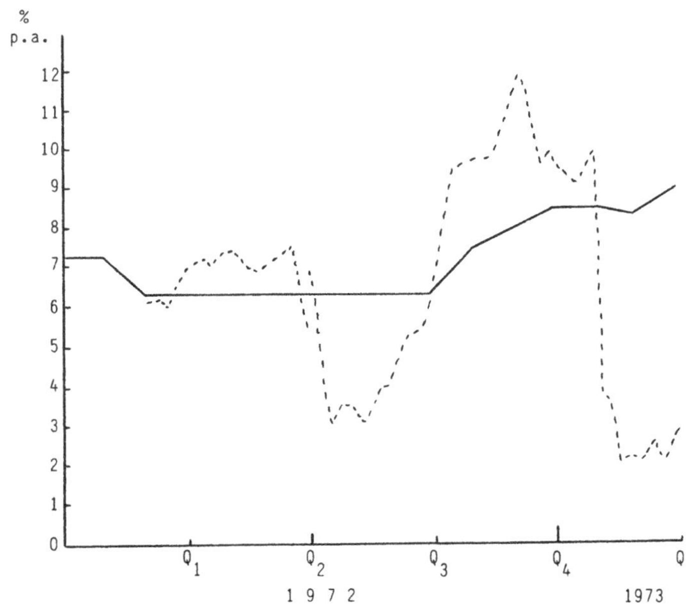

——— Domestic Deutsche Mark prime lending rate

------- Three-month inter-bank Euro-Deutsche Mark rate plus 1% spread plus:
40% cash deposit ratio March 1st - June 30th
50% cash deposit ratio July 1st - March 31st

Sources: <u>BIS Annual Report</u>, 1973

<u>World Financial Markets</u>, April 1973

The devaluation of the dollar and the abandonment of fixed exchange rates resulted not from the Euro-dollar market's possessing so much power that it was unilaterally able to breach European capital controls, but rather from the inherent weaknesses and deficiencies of the controls themselves. Indeed, short of proscribing capital flows entirely, it is difficult to see how destabilising capital movements could have been effectively eliminated within the existing framework of misaligned parities and fixed exchange rates.[3]

THE CHANGING PATTERN OF MARKET ACTIVITY

The events of the late sixties and early seventies reorientated market activity in several ways:

Declining Lending Margins

The slowing and eventual reversal of US banks' Euro-dollar borrowing left the market with excess banking capacity and a high degree of liquidity. These problems were compounded by the competitive activities of consortium banks -- whose accelerated formation was a response to the developing fashion for syndicated medium-term credits -- and Japanese banks who, as relative newcomers, undercut market rates to become established as rapidly as possible. These competitive pressures prompted a marked narrowing of lending margins, with spreads declining to levels as low as $\frac{3}{8}$% over LIBOR[4] for prime non-bank borrowers and 1% over LIBOR for other borrowers. Compared to the 2% - 2½% spreads of earlier years, these margins were often insufficient to provide an adequate return on capital, even without taking into account the effects of inflation.

Lengthening Credit Maturities

A further consequence of the intensification of competitive pressures was a significant lengthening of medium-term credit maturities. Originally intended to embrace periods of three to five years, "medium-term" increasingly began to apply to credits with longer maturities until eventually, in the first half of 1974, it came to include credits with maturities exceeding fifteen years such as the $30 million, nineteen-year Philippine

National Bank credit issued in early 1974. Euro-dollar credits thus became available which were not only larger but also had longer maturities than comparable long-term financing instruments such as Euro-bonds. This lengthening of maturities was also accompanied by rapid growth in the volume of medium-term facilities, which increased from $4.7 billion in 1970 to $21.9 billion in 1973 (table 9), although this growth was abruptly curtailed in the latter half of 1974 when, following the crisis of confidence, new credits declined from $19.9 billion in the first half to $9.4 billion in the second half of the year.

Expansion and Diversification of Medium-Term Lending

The proliferation of capital controls and the intensification of competition obliged banks to extend existing Euro-dollar facilities and develop new outlets to meet global lending targets.

One way in which this was achieved was through increased lending to less-developed countries (LDCs) which prior to the seventies had been considered of marginal commercial interest. Indeed, as late as 1970, LDCs accounted for only $0.3 billion (6%) of total publicised medium-term credits (table 9), but in the following year lending to these countries began to accelerate and eventually reached a rate of just under $9 billion per annum in the first half of 1974.

This expansion was accompanied by more diversified lending, particularly to the governments and public sector authorities of Western European nations such as Italy and the UK. The major stimulus to increased UK public sector borrowing was the reinstatement, in the March 1973 budget, of the Treasury Exchange Rate Guarantee under which the Treasury provided exchange rate guarantees for dollar borrowing by nationalised industries and local authorities[5] for periods of five years or over.[6] The facility was extended in October 1973 to include credits denominated in currencies other than the dollar, whilst the minimum period for which foreign currencies could be borrowed for domestic purposes was reduced from five to two years.[7] The relaxation of these restrictions contributed to a $2.6 billion increase in UK public sector net foreign currency borrowing in 1973.

Balance of payments considerations also figured prominently in the Italian authorities' decision to encourage public and semi-public bodies to resort to external borrowing for domestic financing purposes and to surrender the proceeds to the official reserves -- a policy which contributed to Italian medium-term foreign currency credits' increasing from $0.9 billion in 1972 to $4.8 billion in 1973.

The combined effect of UK and Italian borrowing was to contribute to an increase not only in total medium-term credits -- which accelerated from $6.8 billion in 1972 to $21.9 billion in 1973 (table 9) -- but also in the size of individual credits, which finally reached the $1 billion level in the first half of 1973 when the British Electricity Council negotiated a $1 billion ten-year syndicated credit. Once the precedent had been established, there was a succession of billion dollar credits for Italian public sector agencies -- credits which were to pave the way for the multi-billion dollar payments financings of 1974.

NOTES

1. Report of the Deutsche Bundesbank (1972), p.5.

2. Ceilings on multiple-maturity time deposits of $100,000 or more were suspended on July 16th 1973 when the distinction between single- and multiple-maturity deposits was abandoned. Ceilings on deposits of less than $100,000 remained in operation, however.

3. An attempt at identifying, isolating and preventing speculative inflows was undertaken by the Swiss authorities in August 1971. The attempt involved the major Swiss banks' limiting the conversion into free Swiss francs of US dollar inflows which appeared to be of a speculative nature to $2 million per customer per day when the exchange rate fell below 3.96 francs and to $1 million per customer per day when it fell to, or below 3.95 francs. The measure was of limited success, however, and was abandoned with the implementation of the Smithsonian Agreement.

4. LIBOR is defined and explained in Appendix A, p.128.

5. Public sector bodies were free to borrow without exchange cover, subject to Treasury approval.

6. The facility had been restricted to borrowings of ten years and over in July 1971, and withdrawn entirely in March 1972.

7. The initial five-year restriction had been introduced in January 1971 to curb capital inflows.

Chapter Seven

THE 1974 OIL CRISIS

1974 was the most turbulent year in Euro-dollar market history, as the market suffered and then recovered from visible retrenchment following an initial period of rapid growth prompted by a fourfold increase in the price of oil.

The quadrupling of oil prices between October 1973 and January 1974 precipitated an unprecedented transfer of wealth from consumers to producers and confronted the international monetary system in general and western economies in particular with the twin problems of accommodating this transfer and financing the resultant payments deficits.

The three principal channels through which such flows could have been accommodated were the US banking system, reserve adjustments and the Euro-dollar market. The US banking system was physically capable of accommodating these flows, but its contribution was limited by the political reluctance of producer nations to deposit revenues directly with a country which was itself the subject of an oil embargo.[1] The use of reserve adjustments, on the other hand, was limited by the quantitative inadequacy of global exchange reserves and by the deflationary consequences of this means of financing for consumer nations. The Euro-dollar market, in contrast, possessed both the financial capacity and the political acceptability to recycle deposits from producers to consumers and thus played a pre-eminent role in the financing of the 1974 oil crisis.

DEMAND DEVELOPMENTS

The role of recycling surpluses from producers

to consumers was technically no different from that which the market had performed since the late fifties, although an increase in the size of individual credits and a lengthening of maturity transformations had been necessitated by the crisis. Where a marked disparity between the market's pre- and post-oil crisis financing roles emerged, however, was in terms of the strategic economic and political importance with which this latter role came to be regarded, for not only did the market's recycling of surpluses enable consumer nations to finance their deficits and continue pursuing policies of "full employment" -- thereby avoiding the necessity of adopting deflationary measures --, it also contributed to the avoidance of the political crises and even military confrontations which might have ensued from a situation in which consumer nations were denied access to oil supplies, either because they lacked the resources necessary to finance these purchases or because producers were unwilling to accept these resources either as a medium of payment or as a store of wealth. The strategic importance of this role was clearly demonstrated by the rapid transition from a situation in which the attitudes and measures adopted by the monetary authorities in the early seventies were hostile and inimical to the market's continued development, to one in which the authorities not only condoned Euro-dollar borrowing but also made active recourse to Euro-dollars on their own account.

Amongst the more notable countries resorting to the Euro-dollar market for payments financing purposes were France, Italy, Japan, -- which were heavily dependent on imported energy supplies -- and the UK which, although less dependent on oil, was obliged to resort to Euro-dollars to finance what had already developed into a chronically weak pre-oil crisis payments position.

The first large-scale borrower to emerge was France, which announced in January 1974 that the Société Générale was arranging a $1.5 billion credit which would finance approximately one-third of the Republic's estimated current account deficit for 1974. Whilst this loan was not drawn on in 1974, the fact that the market possessed the capacity to provide a credit of this magnitude, especially in the wake of the billion dollar credits of 1973, was testimony to its unique depth and flexibility as an international capital market.

This credit was soon overshadowed, however, by what was to amount to the largest single credit ever raised in the Euro-dollar market when, in the UK budget of 1974, it was announced that in conjunction with the Bank of England the London clearing banks had arranged a $2.5 billion credit for the UK government. The credit had a ten year revolving maturity based on roll-over periods of three, six or twelve months, with spreads over the respective LIBORs of $\frac{3}{8}$% for the first two years, $\frac{1}{2}$% for the next three years, $\frac{5}{8}$% for the following two years and $\frac{3}{4}$% for the final three years. In marked contrast to the French loan, the credit was rapidly utilised, with the entire $2.5 billion being drawn between October 1974 and February 1975. The credit represented a landmark in the history of the Euro-dollar market, for not only did it constitute the largest single facility ever arranged but, following so soon after the French $1.5 billion credit, it proved conclusively that the Euro-dollar market possessed both the political ability and the financial capacity to accommodate what effectively amounted to the wholesale financing of national payments deficits.

The market's willingness to provide such facilities, however, was not so readily extended to the third major borrower, Italy, which encountered increasing difficulty in its attempts to secure credits beyond the $7.4 billion of medium-term facilities it had already negotiated in the four years up to December 1973. The size of this debt (the largest of its kind outstanding at the end of 1973) and the increasing concern over Italy's deteriorating payments position and ability to service this debt, limited the extent to which the market was prepared to continue financing Italy's payments deficits. This reluctance was notable because it represented the first occasion on which a European country had encountered serious difficulty in the securing of further Euro-dollar facilities, and because the collective market decision that Italy had essentially exhausted her borrowing capacity and that further facilities should be witheld was indicative of the responsibility and underlying financial integrity with which the market discharged its lending obligations. Indeed this assessment of Italy's borrowing capacity was subsequently vindicated by the declaration of the US Comptroller of Currency that Italy's medium- and long-term loans were problematical, and by the fact that Italy was, in the absence of alternative facilities, compelled to secure a $2 billion bilateral loan from the Bundesbank, in return for which she was obliged to pledge as collateral approximately 20% of her gold reserves.

The substantial Euro-dollar borrowing resorted to by France, Italy and the UK contributed to a significant increase in the size of individual credits and the total value of Euro-dollar facilities, and to a pronounced lengthening of the maturities for which longer-term credits became available. In the first half of 1974, publicly-announced medium-term credit facilities (principally dollar-denominated) increased by $19.9 billion, approximately 25% of which was accounted for in the first quarter of the year by credits with maturities of ten years or more (table 10). Within this overall increase, approximately $9.7 billion (49%) was accounted for by the public utilities and government and public financial institutions of industrial countries (table 11).

Medium-term facilities were not the only form of financing resorted to by consumer nations, however, for a considerable volume of assistance was provided directly through the inter-bank sector of the Euro-dollar market. The most significant borrower in this respect was Japan, whose net liabilities to reporting banks increased by a substantial $5.4 billion in the first half of 1974 (medium-term credits, in contrast, increased by a negligible $0.2 billion to reach $0.5 billion by the end of June 1974). This inflow was remarkable not only because of its size and the speed with which it was effected, but also because it represented claims which had been fully transacted, unlike medium-term credits which, once negotiated, may remain as undrawn, contingent facilities.

Japan's heavy dependence on short-term, inter-bank Euro-dollar credits was not without cost, however, for as Japanese liabilities increased and began to approach the lending limits which banks impose on other banks, both individually and collectively, the margin over LIBOR at which Japanese banks could secure credits was subjected to increasing pressure until banks were eventually required to pay spreads in excess of 2% p.a. over LIBOR. At this point the Japanese authorities instructed banks to curtail their exposure to Euro-dollars to prevent any further deterioration in their borrowing status and the emergence of a situation in which the Euro-dollar market itself might deny Japanese banks further access to Euro-dollar resources. The effect of this curtailment was dramatic, with reporting banks' dollar claims on Japan increasing by only $0.8 billion in the second half of 1974, compared to $6.2 billion in the first half of the year (table 12).

Developed countries were not the only borrowers to resort to Euro-dollar financing, for the net absorption of Euro-dollars by countries outside the reporting area (excluding Japan) amounted to $20 billion in 1974 (table 12), $8 billion of which was supplied by the inside reporting area itself. The Euro-dollar market's role as a net supplier of funds as well as a recycling mechanism thus extended well beyond the developed countries of the inside reporting area.

SUPPLY DEVELOPMENTS

Just as the large-scale demands for deficit financing by consumer nations had threatened to impose a severe burden on the international monetary system, so the existence of highly liquid and volatile payments surpluses threatened to impose similar burdens on the system's capacity to absorb and recycle these funds. The basic problem arose from producers' inability to spend all, or even a significant proportion of their newly acquired wealth and from the need to recycle these surpluses to consumer nations if global deflation was to be averted. It was a problem compounded, moreover, by the conflicting interests of producers and consumers, with producers seeking to maintain their reserves in highly liquid and relatively risk-free forms, whilst consumers sought to finance their deficits on a medium- to long-term basis. The successful accommodation of the oil crisis thus required both the recycling of surpluses from producers to consumers and the transformation of these surpluses from short-term deposits into longer-term credits.

The Euro-dollar market played a pre-eminent role in the absorption and transformation of these surpluses which, for the oil-producing exporting countries collectively, amounted to approximately $56 billion in 1974. The deployment of these surpluses is illustrated in table 13, which shows that the Euro-currency (predominantly Euro-dollar) market attracted the largest single share of surpluses, although this share was not evenly distributed throughout the year:

In the first quarter of 1974, the accumulation of producers' surpluses amounted to a modest $7 billion, of which $2.5 billion (36%) was accounted for by non-deposit investments. The remaining $4.5 billion represented bank deposits, of which $2.5 billion (36%) was accounted for by foreign currency deposits in London and $1.5 billion (21%) by foreign currency deposits in other centres. Dollar deposits in the US, in contrast, increased by a modest $0.6 billion whilst sterling deposits in the UK actually declined by $0.1 billion. The Euro-currency market thus accounted for approximately half of the total deployment of oil producers' surpluses in the first quarter of 1974.

This pattern was essentially repeated in the second quarter of the year although the magnitudes involved were considerably larger, with the total surplus more than doubling to $15.5 billion, $8 billion (52%) of which was accounted for by foreign currency deposits, the greater part of which ($4.5 billion) was deposited in London. (Dollar deposits in the US and sterling deposits in the UK, in contrast, recorded a combined increase of just $1.5 billion, which was insufficient to account for more than 10% of total investments). In the first half of 1974, therefore, foreign currency deposits, principally dollar-denominated, accounted for $12 billion (53%) of total producer surpluses.

This pattern was not repeated in the third quarter of 1974, when the undermining of producers' confidence in the market occasioned a diversification of surpluses away from Euro-currency deposits to more traditional forms of investment offering greater security and comparable liquidity. This resulted in the deceleration of foreign currency deposits in London and elsewhere from $8 billion in the second quarter of 1974 to $4.9 billion in the third quarter of the year and in an acceleration of dollar deposits in the US and sterling deposits in the UK from $1.5 billion to $3.4 billion over the same period.

The restoration of confidence and more

normal trading conditions in the final quarter of 1974 reversed this downward trend and new foreign currency deposits recovered from $4.9 billion (30%) in the third quarter to $5.9 billion (34%) in the final quarter of the year. This increase contrasted with a significant reversal to a mere $0.3 billion (2%) in the volume of dollar and sterling funds flowing to the US and UK markets respectively.

The Euro-dollar market thus proved the largest single repository for producer surpluses in 1974, with foreign currency deposits accounting for $22.8 billion (41%) of total producer surpluses -- London alone accounted for $13.8 billion (25%) of this total -- within which reporting banks' aggregate dollar liabilities to the Middle East increased by $17.8 billion. In discharging this role, however, the market was confronted with a number of serious problems:

Firstly, the substantial degree of maturity transformation required to convert producer deposits into consumer credits subjected the Euro-dollar market's maturity structure to considerable pressure. From March 1974 onwards, all London Euro-currency net lending for six months and over was financed with net liabilities with maturities of less than six months, whilst for the medium-term Euro-currency market as a whole, medium-term credits with maturities of seven years and over accounted for a substantial 76% of all medium-term credits announced in 1974.

Secondly, the unequal distribution of investment surpluses amongst Euro-banks, caused by producers' attempts to maximise security and liquidity by discriminating amongst banks and confining investments to a handful of the world's largest international banks, created problems for both the market collectively and banks individually. [2] At a collective level, the high degree of deposit concentration posed a threat to market confidence -- a threat which assumed particularly menacing dimensions in the second half of 1974 and subjected the market to considerable pressure. At an individual level, producer discrimination resulted in declining capital deposit ratios and increased supply vicissitudes as producer disaffection with one or more recipient banks interrupted the intermediation of deposits to secondary banks.

The depositing of a substantial volume of producer surpluses in the Euro-dollar market thus confronted the market with the twin problems of transforming these deposits from short-term producer liabilities into longer-term consumer claims and of correcting the distributional imbalances resulting from the concentration of these deposits on a selected few of the world's leading international banks. The market overcame these problems but, in so doing, was subjected to increasing strains and grew progressively more reluctant to continue accepting deposits both on the same terms and on the same scale as previously -- a reluctance which, in conjunction with the subsequent crisis of confidence, resulted in a widening of the dispersion of market interest rates and the creation of refinancing problems for banks with less than prime status.

CHANGES IN CAPITAL CONTROLS

The oil crisis also exerted an indirect impact on the Euro-dollar market by occasioning changes in the international pattern of capital controls. These changes were significant for not only did they stimulate the flow of new deposits to the Euro-dollar market, they also regenerated deposit demand from European sources which a succession of post-1971 controls had sought to progressively disfranchise. The changes represented the dismantling of the intricate network of capital controls which had been assiduously assembled in increasingly futile attempts to avert the destabilising capital inflows of the early seventies, and their replacing by a policy of capital mobility which, it was hoped, would stimulate capital inflows and provide the resources necessary to finance prospective payments deficits. Two distinct patterns of changes are discernible: US changes stimulated a substantial outflow of capital from the US which augmented the potential supply of Euro-dollar deposits, whilst European changes promoted capital inflows and thereby stimulated the demand for Euro-dollars.

US Changes

The Nixon administration announced on December 26th 1973 that a significant easing of capital controls would take effect from January 1st 1974.[3] The changes subsequently announced on January 29th, however, were the most significant since the introduction of IET for, with immediate effect: the Interest Equalization Tax was reduced to zero; Foreign Direct Investment controls were abolished and the Voluntary Foreign Credit Restraint Program was terminated.

The relaxation of these controls was undertaken to permit the smooth recycling of producer surpluses and, because of the expected demand for dollar investments, to avoid any excessive appreciation of the dollar which would have eroded the benefits of the two dollar devaluations of 1971 and 1973. The impact on US capital outflows for 1974 as a whole was dramatic: US direct investment abroad accelerated to $7.3 billion, foreign bond issues in the US almost doubled to $2.4 billion and US banks' foreign claims more than tripled to $19.3 billion.

At a stroke, therefore, the barriers which had impeded the free outflow of US capital in the sixties and seventies had been dismantled and the potential supply of Euro-dollar deposits significantly augmented.

European Changes

Changes in European capital controls, in contrast, were intended to promote the inflow rather than the outflow of capital and avoid the emergence of acute deflationary pressures. The changes principally involved:

-- the suspension of both negative interest rates and proscribed interest payments on non-resident liabilities;

-- the reduction or elimination of reserve ratios on non-resident liabilities;

-- the abolition of the "O-guilder" circuit and dual exchange markets such as those for the lira and French franc;

-- the removal of restrictions on non-residents' purchases of domestic securities and real-estate;

-- the restoration of freedom to resort to overseas borrowing, which was subsequently generally encouraged;

-- the reimposition of restrictions on foreign lending in domestic currencies which further favoured the growth of the Euro-dollar market.

Changes in European capital controls were thus clearly designed to promote capital inflows. In the process, however, they also freed the Euro-dollar market from the succession of administrative constraints which had served to potentially disfranchise Europe as an outlet for Euro-dollar deposits.

An indication of the extent to which changes in capital controls facilitated the recycling of producer surpluses as opposed to the reserve financing of consumer deficits -- and a further indication, therefore, of the importance of the Euro-dollar market's recycling role -- may be derived from the composition and distribution of international reserves in 1974 (table 14). Despite the severe shock administered to the international monetary system by the rise in oil prices, the distribution of international reserves remained remarkably stable. The largest collective distributional change (excluding oil-exporting countries) was a mere 12% decline in the reserves of more developed primary producing countries whilst industrial countries, which might have been expected to have sustained severe reserve losses in 1974 as a result of payments financing difficulties, similarly recorded only marginal changes amounting to a reserve gain of 4%. Nor was this stability achieved at the expense of any untoward sectoral decline in the composition of international reserves, for every reserve category recorded an increase in 1974, the largest of which was identified holdings of Euro-dollars which accounted for $14.9 billion (42%) of the total $36 billion increase in reserves.

That international reserves should have exhibited such stability in the face of acute payments financing difficulties was testimony to the Euro-dollar market's remarkable ability to absorb and recycle surpluses from producers to consumers, thereby financing the latters' deficits and obviating the need for the deflationary measures which might otherwise have been necessitated.

NOTES

1. Oil exports to the US were embargoed between November 1973 and March 1974.

2. A measure of the degree of distributional deposit inequality for the London Euro-currency market as a whole in 1975 is indicated by the fact that twenty-one banks (6%) accounted for $82 billion (49%) of total market deposits, whilst at the other extreme one hundred and twenty-five banks (38%) accounted for just 1% of total deposits. Whilst the whole of this inequality cannot be attributed solely to producer surpluses, it is clear that the selective depositing of producer reserves accentuated deposit inequalities and intensified the problems of reserve recycling.

3. The easing of capital controls principally provided for a reduction in IET from 0.75% to 0.25% and the extensive relaxation of both FDIP restrictions and VFCRP guidelines.

Chapter Eight

THE CRISIS OF CONFIDENCE

The second half of 1974 was characterised by a significant decline in Euro-dollar positions. Despite the market's smooth and efficient recycling of producer surpluses, an element of disquiet at the continuing trend of Euro-dollar activity had begun to emerge by late spring and had contributed to some initial consolidation of Euro-dollar positions. The subsequent mishandling by the German authorities of the closure of a relatively obscure German bank succeeded in transforming this consolidation into the worst crisis in the history of the Euro-dollar market.

The immediate cause of this initial disquiet was not attributable to any one factor but rather to the cumulative impact of a combination of technical and general factors which were frequently beyond the immediate control of the market.

One of the more disquieting technical features of the oil crisis was the steady and often marked decline in banks' capital deposit ratios occasioned not only by the unequal distribution of producer deposits but also by the depressed state of equity and bond markets which precluded the reinforcing of capital structures through the injection of fresh risk/loan capital.

The substantial degree of maturity transformation undertaken by the market in 1974 was a second cause for concern, focused principally on the size of individual credits intermediated and mismatched, which were the largest in the market's history, the magnitude of the maturity transformation undertaken, which was considerably larger in size and volume than anything which the market had previously undertaken, and the distribution of this transformation, which exposed banks to the twin problems of deposit withdrawals and the risks of loan default arising from the concentration of medium-term lending on a small number of high-debt countries such as Italy and the UK (publicly-announced medium-term credit facilities to these two countries amounted to $17.9 billion by mid-1974 and represented 38% of total non-US facilities extended since 1970).

A third factor undermining confidence was uncertainty over the financing of existing debt obligations. Developing countries figured prominently in such anxieties, although the very high level of obligations incurred by developed countries also proved a serious source of concern. Such misgivings were principally concentrated on Italy and came to the fore when a combination of heavy Italian medium-term borrowing ($9.7 billion in the four and a half years to mid-1974) and a growing payments imbalance contributed to the market's refusal to finance more than $500 million of the $1.2 billion Mediobanca loan.

A final technical factor to intensify disquiet, embracing elements of the previous factors, was the absence of a formal "lender of last resort". Whilst this "weakness" had always been considered more apparent than real, it assumed particularly menacing dimensions in 1974 when the risk of a series of debt defaults threatened to precipitate a domino-style collapse. Fears of such a collapse sought expression at both a developed- and less-developed country level. In the former case, anxiety was partly dispelled by the size of individual countries' reserves and by the unwinding of inter-bank positions vis-à-vis the individual countries concerned. In the case of less-developed countries, however, no such safeguards were forthcoming, for not only were individual exchange reserves generally insufficient to provide more than token debt support, but inter-bank claims on these countries were also limited. The prospect of global deflation, moreover, threatened to exacerbate the payments difficulties which these countries were already facing as a result of the oil crisis.

At a general level, concern was expressed at the rapid increase in interest rates (three-month Euro-dollar deposits increased from 8.6% to 12.4% between March and June 1974) which threatened to presage the onset of a severe liquidity squeeze. This was disquieting not only because of the financing difficulties which would have been created but also, paradoxically, because of the increased Euro-dollar liquidity which would have been occasioned by the stimulation of further inflows of short-term dollar deposits. Banks were thus confronted with the prospect of paying high short-term rates to finance medium- to long-term portfolios whilst short-term liquidity continued to increase and inflate an already liquid deposit base.

A second factor to contribute to the prevailing climate of uncertainty was the belief that the oil crisis was a purely transitory phenomenon and that Euro-dollar credits could continue to be used to maintain pre-crisis domestic consumption levels. This attitude contrasted sharply with that of the Euro-dollar market which regarded the credits as a purely temporary palliative, affording relief only until more permanent recycling facilities could be instituted. In many respects this conflict of attitudes represented one of the more disconcerting features of the crisis, demonstrating as it did the conceptual gulf which existed between borrowers and lenders.

By the end of the first half of 1974,therefore, it had become apparent that there would be no retreat on the oil prices front and that, whereas the deposit intermediation and maturity transformation undertaken by the market in previous years had served to promote the relatively slow process of economic growth, the demands confronting the market in 1974 were of an entirely different nature and magnitude, involving the accommodation of the much faster and more unbalanced growth of some of the world's largest payments imbalances. Some reappraisal of the market's recycling role had thus become inevitable.

THE CRISIS

The inevitable reappraisal of the market's recycling role came sooner rather than later and was precipitated, almost accidentally, by the closure of the German I.D. Herstatt bank. Although the crisis of the bank's closure was one of the shortest in the market's history and might easily have proved one of the least significant, events conspired to ensure that it exerted the most contractionary impact the Euro-dollar market had hitherto experienced.

The immediate cause of the crisis was the announcement of the perfunctory closure of the Cologne bank I.D. Herstatt on Wednesday June 26th by order of the Bundesbank and the West German Control Board for Credit. It was not the magnitude of the bank's foreign exchange losses which sent powerful shock waves reverberating through the markets (since the extent of these losses was not known at the time), but rather the manner in which the closure was handled. The decision to close the bank in the middle of a working day, whilst transactions were still in the process of being executed, resulted in a large number of transactions remaining uncompleted and the generation of substantial market losses, the most notable of which was the $10 million loss incurred by the UK merchant bank Hill Samuel through an incomplete foreign exchange transaction.

The implications of the manner in which the Herstatt closure was handled were alarming for both individual institutions and the foreign exchange and Euro-dollar markets as a whole, for they raised the spectre of future mid-working day closures and the prospect of further substantial losses. The fact, moreover, that the Herstatt closure followed so soon after the collapse of the US National Bank of San Diego and the losses sustained by the United California Bank in Basel, US Franklin National Bank, Westdeutsche Landesbank and the Union Bank of Switzerland, as well as the secondary banking crisis in the UK, intensified fears of a domino-style banking collapse, renewed exchange controls and a Euro-dollar liquidity crisis.

It was the mishandling of the Herstatt closure, therefore, and the precedent which this established, rather than the size of the foreign exchange losses incurred, that occasioned an international crisis whose repercussions proved out of all proportion to the magnitude of the losses involved. The realisation, moreover, that such a closure was possible and that Euro-dollar transactions might, in such a situation, remain uncompleted precipitated a fundamental reappraisal of market activity.

REPERCUSSIONS OF THE CRISIS

Decline in Euro-dollar Positions

The most severe impact of the crisis was experienced at the level of inter-bank positions, which declined by an absolute $5.2 billion from assets of $122.9 billion at the end of June to assets of $117.7 billion by the end of September 1974 (table 7(ii)). This decline was the largest recorded in the market's history and forcefully demonstrated not only the erosion of confidence occasioned by the crisis, but also the fear of a domino-style banking collapse -- a fear which was clearly expressed in the market's attitude to Italy, whose deteriorating payments position compelled Italian banks to pay an increasingly high premium over LIBOR to secure inter-bank credits. This effectively absorbed the spread which Italian banks could earn on inter-bank trading and contributed to a dramatic reversal of the growth of Italian banks' positions vis-à-vis the Euro-dollar market, whose aggregate claims on Italy, having increased by $5.8 billion in the second half of 1973, declined by a substantial $2.6 billion in the second half of 1974.

In contrast to the absolute decline in positions vis-à-vis banks, positions vis-à-vis non-banks were less severely affected by the crisis and consequently experienced only a relative decline in growth, with liabilities increasing by a modest $270 million and claims remaining essentially unchanged in the third quarter of 1974 (tables 7(i) and 7(ii)). The greater stability of these positions emphasised the asymmetrical nature of the crisis, which was concentrated principally on inter-bank rather than non-bank activities. The non-bank community did not remain entirely impervious to developments within the banking sector of the market, however, for the increased risk with which Euro-dollar deposits were perceived by the oil producers occasioned a substantial diversification of producer investments away from the Euro-currency markets to more traditional repositories of wealth such as the US. This resulted in a deceleration of producers' foreign currency deposits from increases of $8 billion to $4.9 billion between the second and third quarters of 1974 and an acceleration of dollar deposits in the US from increases of $0.8 billion to $2.3 billion over the same period (table 13).

Increased Amplitude of Euro-dollar Interest Rates

A second consequence of the crisis was an increase in the amplitude of the tiered structure of market interest rates. This reflected the increased spreads (risk premiums) which selected banks were required to pay to secure funds on the inter-bank market and the reduced rates (security discount) which prime banks had to pay to attract deposits.

The risk premium was a response to the general lack of market confidence and involved banks both individually and collectively. At an individual level, fears were principally focused on the possibility that a small bank might find itself in difficulties and might lack the reserves necessary to sustain such losses. Concern was also expressed at the possibility of collective defaults occasioned either by trading difficulties or by the imposition of administrative constraints such as exchange controls.

Amongst those banks generating the greatest disquiet were Italian and Japanese banks which had both resorted extensively to Euro-dollar facilities -- the former for inter-bank arbitraging and the latter for domestic financing purposes --, but which were causing concern for two quite different reasons. In the case of Italian banks, the high level of public-sector foreign-currency borrowing and the deteriorating payments position were threatening the Italian economy with debt-servicing difficulties, whilst in the case of Japanese banks it was feared that the extensive recourse to Euro-dollar borrowing might necessitate the introduction of capital controls to curb subsequent capital outflows. The disquiet generated by these possibilities manifested itself in a substantial risk premium, often as high as 2% over LIBOR, which Italian and Japanese banks were required to pay to secure funds in the inter-bank market. This eventually resulted in a voluntary withdrawal of Italian banks and an enforced withdrawal of Japanese banks (at the instigation of Japanese authorities) from the inter-bank market.

The market's security discount, in contrast, proved less significant, since its impact was confined to those prime banks whose size and status enabled them to offer rates below the market average to secure deposits. The discount was prompted essentially by banks' own desire to curb the prodigious inflows of deposits which were contributing to the decline in capital deposit ratios and to the deterioration in maturity structures. The effect of the discount was to sharpen the distinction between prime and non-prime banks and to contribute to the rechannelling of deposits from the Euro-dollar market to the US and other centres.

Increased Euro-dollar Interest Rate Differentials

A third consequence of the crisis was the emergence of a substantial Euro-dollar/US CD interest rate differential in favour of Euro-dollars. This differential widened from close to zero in April to approach 200 basis points per annum within a few days of the onset of the crisis in June. Such levels had been previously recorded only in exceptional circumstances such as the sustained Euro-dollar borrowings of 1969 and the dollar crises of 1971 and 1973 and, although they subsequently retreated, they nevertheless remained in excess of 100 basis points throughout most of the summer months, narrowing only with the emergence of a decline in US interest rates in September and the gradual restoration of market confidence. The differential reflected increased fears of a liquidity crisis -- prompted in part by foreign exchange losses, high interest rates and the risk of wholesale deposit withdrawals in the event of oil-exporting countries' losing confidence in the market -- and the possible reintroduction of exchange controls which would have affected the Euro-dollar market through constraints on capital flows.

Transition from Borrowers' to Lenders' Market

A fourth repercussion of the crisis was the rapid transition from a borrowers' to a lenders' market which occasioned major changes in both the market's mode of operation and its profile. The intense competition which had characterised Euro-dollar lending in the period immediately preceding the crisis evaporated almost overnight, with banks expressing reluctance to extend credits to less than first-class names and to participate in loans with spreads of less than 1%. This raised spreads on prime credits to an average $1\frac{1}{4}$% from previous lows of $\frac{3}{8}$% and also confronted final borrowers with the prospect of securing loans at disproportionately higher levels of LIBOR since spreads on inter-bank credits had also widened. The maturities on which LIBOR spreads were based were also shortened from the previously common six months to three months and even one month, thus ensuring that banks were able to recoup increased financing costs more rapidly.

The effect of these changes on the market's profile was to increase lending selectivity and to "crowd out" those fringe borrowers whose financing needs might, in earlier years, have been accommodated by the market.

Reduced Maturity and Value of Credits

A further consequence of the crisis was a marked and rapid reduction in the maturity and total value of new medium-term credit facilities. Between the second and third quarters of 1974, the differential share of total publicly-announced medium-term credit facilities accounted for by maturities of less than seven years and seven to less than ten years narrowed from 7% and 85% to 37% and 45% respectively (table 10). Comparable reductions were also recorded in the value of new medium-term credit facilities which declined from $19.9 billion in the first half of 1974 -- a level which almost equalled the $21.9 billion recorded for the whole of 1973 -- to just $9.4 billion in the latter half of the year.

Increased Dollar Share of Euro-currency Positions

A sixth repercussion of the crisis was an increase in the dollar's share of Euro-currency positions. This increase was essentially a response to the lack of confidence prevailing in the Euro-currency market and was accounted for not only by the fact that the greater portion of oil-exporting countries' Euro-currency investments was dollar-denominated (reporting banks' non-dollar liabilities to the Middle East increased by a modest $1.8 billion from $4.1 billion at the end of 1973 to $5.9 billion at the end of 1974), but also by the more important fact that the Euro-dollar market possessed greater depth, resilience and flexibility than the non-dollar sector of the market and was consequently better placed to weather the crisis of confidence.

This was reflected in a two percentage points increase in the dollar's average share of the Euro-currency market (assets plus liabilities) from 70% at the end of 1973 to 72% by the end of 1974.

Consortium Bank Retrenchment

The final repercussion of significance was the contractionary impact exerted on individual categories of banks. The most severely affected were consortium banks, whose structure rendered them particularly susceptible to adverse shifts in market sentiment. This susceptibility resulted firstly from the fact that, since consortium banks' predominant shareholders were other banks (none of which generally held a majority share), it was feared that in the event of trading difficulties assistance would be no more readily forthcoming from these banks than from the central banks of the countries concerned. Secondly, and of greater concern, was the maturity structure of consortium banks' Euro-currency positions, not because this structure was technically weaker than that of the market as a whole but rather because it was potentially weaker. Consortium banks lacked branch networks and were therefore unable to cultivate strong deposit bases. Since they consequently had to depend for deposits on the inter-bank market, which was most severely affected by the crisis of confidence, they faced the twin problems of potential deposit withdrawals and difficulty in securing further or, even more seriously, replacement financing. Consortium banks were thus more exposed to, and suffered more acutely from the vicissitudes of market confidence -- a fact reflected in the retrenchment which they experienced between March and November 1974, when their share of total London Euro-currency claims declined from 8.1% ($12.1 billion) to 6.7% ($10.4 billion).

The crisis of confidence engendered by the Herstatt affair thus exerted a contractionary impact both on banks individually and on the market collectively. The crisis was not entirely pernicious, however, for it occasioned two developments which were tantamount to the establishment of "lender of last resort" facilities:

Firstly, at the September meeting of the

central bank governors of the Group of Ten, it was formally announced that the central banks were willing, should the need arise, to provide facilities necessary to prevent the emergence of an international liquidity crisis and to assist the international banking community to overcome any temporary liquidity shortfalls which might arise from factors such as the withdrawal of producer surpluses.

Secondly, and in close succession to these guarantees, the Bank of England announced that it had secured undertakings from consortium banks' shareholders that they would provide support facilities for their banks should the need arise -- undertakings which, although not legally enforceable, nevertheless constituted a firm moral commitment to provide assistance should circumstances so dictate.

These guarantees and undertakings established, for the first time in the history of the Euro-dollar market, central bank responsibility for the provision of facilities to avert international liquidity crises and, by extension, head office responsibility for the actions and policies of overseas branches. These measures, in conjunction with the introduction of more comprehensive reporting requirements and the imposition of limits on individual banks' foreign exchange positions, contributed to the restoration of confidence and normal trading conditions such that by the end of 1974, not only had an earlier third quarter decline in Euro-dollar positions been reversed, but aggregate market liabilities had increased by $25 billion compared to positions outstanding at the beginning of the year.

Thus the market successfully surmounted the worst crisis in its history and emerged not only larger but structurally more resilient.

POST-SCRIPT

If the years of crisis boded ill for the international monetary system, the same cannot be said for their effect on the Euro-dollar market, which emerged from the crises both larger and more resilient than ever.

The opportunity of observing the Euro-dollar market as it functioned within the wider context of the international monetary system was uniquely provided by the crisis years of 1968 - 1974. Such an opportunity is unlikely to arise again in the near future, given the greater flexibility with which international affairs are now conducted and the increased resilience of the system in general. The freezing of Iranian and Argentinian assets in recent years, for example, has done little more than generate financial ripples which the system has readily absorbed.

Gradually, too, the narrower entity which is the Euro-dollar market has been superceded by the all-pervasive global currency market, whilst the emergence in late 1981 of US based International Banking Facilities is, in any case, likely to lure off-shore banking activity back to New York.

Thus the years of crisis may well be over. The global currency market now stands in excess of $1,000 billion, and it remains to be seen what role, if any, the Euro-dollar market will play in future international monetary events.

Appendix A

THE QUANTIFICATION AND INTERPRETATION OF MARKET DATA

The application of the term Euro-dollar to all dollar-denominated and even non-dollar-denominated liabilities reported by banks outside the US is both misleading and inaccurate. That such ambiguity should arise is explained partly by the diverse sources and uses of Euro-dollar deposits and partly by the interrelated, although distinct, roles of the Euro-dollar and foreign exchange markets.

Euro-dollar activity may be defined as:

> The accepting of dollars by banks located in Europe, either through the taking of deposits at Euro-dollar rates of interest or through the swapping of other currencies into dollars, and the onlending of these dollars at Euro-dollar rates of interest to both bank and non-bank borrowers or the use of these dollars by banks on their own account either directly or after swapping into other currencies.

Use of the term Euro-dollar is correctly confined to the transacting of deposits by banks located in the "inside reporting area" of Switzerland and the European Group of Ten countries.[1] This is partly historical, reflecting the geographical distribution of deposits for which the Bank for International Settlements (BIS) first compiled data, and partly in recognition of the potentially greater economic significance of deposits transacted by European banks. Deposits channelled through off-shore staging posts such as Nassau, in contrast, are essentially cosmetic in nature. They are principally undertaken for administrative and taxation purposes and are thus of lesser economic consequence.

An important distinction should also be made between Euro-dollar transactions and other activities involving the dollar. This distinction may best be made by recourse to Euro-dollar interest rates since Euro-dollar transactions, unlike foreign exchange transactions, for example, necessarily involve an interest rate. The most frequently quoted rate is the London Inter-Bank Offer Rate (LIBOR) which is the rate at which prime banks trade deposits in the inter-bank market and which thus acts as a reference rate by which all other rates and lending spreads are determined.

The employment of Euro-dollar deposits as final sources of and uses for domestic and foreign currency swaps should also be explicitly recognised, since these transactions are an important aspect of market activity.

Two basic measures of Euro-dollar activity -- conforming in varying degrees to the definition previously offered -- are available and have been published since 1964 by the BIS.[2] The "gross" measure of market activity is based on the dollar positions of reporting European banks (inside area banks) vis-à-vis bank and non-bank non-residents (tables 7(i) - 7(iii) and 15), while the "net" measure, which is the smaller of the two, represents external dollar positions adjusted to exclude inside area inter-bank activity, include estimated positions vis-à-vis inside area non-bank residents and make allowance for domestic or third-party currency conversions into and out of dollars (table 2).

A third measure of market activity, which is published by the Bank of England, is of lesser definitional conformity since it incorporates both the dollar and non-dollar foreign currency positions of UK banks vis-à-vis resident and non-resident banks and non-banks (table 16).[3] It may be used, however, as a general proxy of the broad magnitude of London Euro-dollar positions since the dollar overwhelmingly dominates Euro-currency activity.

A final measure, which does not conform to the definition previously offered, but to which reference may be made to illustrate the ambiguity of Euro-dollar and Euro-currency positions, is that published by the Morgan Guaranty

Trust Company of New York.[4] This measure is entitled: "Eurocurrency market size" and is based on the foreign currency liabilities and claims of banks in major European countries, the Bahamas, Bahrain, Cayman Islands, Netherlands Antilles, Panama, Canada, Japan, Hong Kong and Singapore. The term "Global currency market" might be more appropriately employed, however, since the series clearly includes the positions of banks located outside the reporting European area.

Although the BIS estimates of gross and net market positions represent the two most acceptable measures of Euro-dollar activity, they should nevertheless be approached with caution and interpreted with care, since they still suffer from a number of conceptual and statistical shortcomings:

The most serious conceptual problem at an aggregate level concerns the question of whether the economic impact of financial markets is more accurately rendered by stock or flow measures of market activity. This assumes particular significance in the case of the Euro-dollar market whose hybrid role emphasises both capital stock and flow functions. Stock estimates of outstanding Euro-dollar claims may constitute an appropriate measure of Euro-dollar capital financing but may prove an equally unreliable indicator of capital flows such as those which arise during periods of currency instability. Flow data, on the other hand, may accurately reflect the velocity of Euro-dollar currency conversions but, by including all financial flows, may distort net capital financing patterns. There is unfortunately no way in which these two functions may be satisfactorily reconciled within the existing framework of Euro-dollar data.

The statistical shortcomings of gross market measures result from:

(i) the inclusion of transactions of both a Euro-dollar and non-Euro-dollar nature, such as US correspondent balances;

(ii) the duplication or double-counting which arises when Euro-dollars are redeposited amongst inside area banks and between inside and outside area banks -- these pyramided deposits constitute a legitimate and indeed fundamental aspect of Euro-dollar activity but nevertheless serve to overstate the volume of final use credit outstanding in the market;[5]

(iii) the exclusion of resident inter-bank and non-bank positions, since these may prove more than just financial and may consequently detract from the full economic impact of gross market estimates;

(iv) the failure to distinguish between deposits converted into and out of non-dollar currencies and deposits accepted from or placed with non-bank residents, preventing the ready identification of Euro-dollars used for speculative and non-speculative purposes;

(v) definitional inconsistencies and reporting discrepancies amongst individual countries, which result in deficiencies in both data comparability and statistical accuracy.

The statistical shortcomings associated with net measures of market activity arise from the statistical complexity of these measures which represent credit created by and channelled through the market and which are derived from reporting banks' external dollar positions adjusted to firstly, exclude liabilities to and claims on the US which may not rightly be considered Euro-dollar transactions; secondly, exclude inside area inter-bank positions except to the extent that some allowance is made for the market's inter-bank money market role; and thirdly, include positions vis-à-vis non-bank residents and conversions both into and out of domestic and third party currencies, effected either through the foreign exchange market or through central bank swap facilities. The resulting sources and uses of funds are then categorised into: inside area sources, consisting of central bank deposits, non-bank deposits irrespective of whether the claimants are resident or non-resident in the country of domicile of the reporting bank and bank deposits of dollars converted out of domestic and third-party currencies; outside area sources, consisting of deposits received from the rest of the world regardless of the domicile or status of the depositor; and inside and outside area uses, consisting of the mirror image of inside and outside area sources.

The statistical shortcomings of these sources and uses result from:

(i) the inclusion of all outside area banks and non-banks as original sources and uses of deposits, since funds may be channelled several times between inside and outside area banks/non-banks without any increase in outstanding credit;

(ii) the inclusion of all inside area non-banks as original sources and uses of deposits, since this too may lead to double-counting and the statistical inflation of outstanding credit;

(iii) the absence of complete data on reporting positions vis-à-vis non-bank residents;

(iv) the double-counting resulting from the inclusion of currency conversions under sources and uses for both Euro-dollars and non-Euro-dollar Euro-currencies;

(v) the exclusion of inside area inter-bank positions, since this may understate the full economic impact of Euro-dollar activity.

Neither gross nor net market estimates, therefore, are entirely satisfactory as measures of Euro-dollar activity. Whilst the former may be used to quantify deposit flows and the latter outstanding credit, both series suffer from statistical and conceptual shortcomings and should thus be applied with caution, any resultant conclusions being interpreted with care.

NOTES

1. Austria, Denmark and Ireland have been included since 1977.

2. Bank for International Settlements Annual Report, Basel, Switzerland.

3. Bank of England Quarterly Bulletin, London, UK.

4. World Financial Markets, New York, U.S.A.

5. The process of pyramided and endogenous Euro-dollar creation is examined in Appendix B, pp. 133-141.

Appendix B

THE CREATION OF EURO-DOLLARS

EURO-DOLLAR CREATION IN THEORY

The creation of Euro-dollars assumes three basic forms which have attracted varying degrees of controversy, not least because of their complex and often interrelated roles.

Primary Euro-dollar Creation

Primary Euro-dollar creation arises when dollar deposits are transferred from US banks to inside area banks and deposited at Euro-dollar rates of interest. These transfers may be undertaken on a voluntary basis, to exploit arbitrage differentials, for example, or for involuntary reasons such as the financing of US balance of payments deficits.

The original dollar deposit may have been held in a variety of forms or acquired in a number of ways:

(i) Dollars might be acquired on a swap basis or purchased in the foreign exchange market. In either case the dollars must have been maintained in the US, since the withdrawal and redepositing of an existing Euro-dollar deposit merely entails a change in deposit ownership with no change in the net volume of deposits outstanding.

(ii) Dollars may be held in "pure" deposit form as private resident or private or official non-resident dollar claims in the US. The distinction between resident and non-resident is of no consequence to the Euro-dollar market although, depending on the measure employed, it may prove of significance in the compilation of US balance of payments measures.

(iii) Dollars may be transferred to the

Euro-dollar market from other off-shore centres such as Nassau.

The process of primary Euro-dollar creation is illustrated in figure B-1 (p. 134), in which the US Bank and the Euro-bank represent the US banking system and the Euro-dollar market respectively. The process might commence when a US resident converts a certificate of deposit, upon its maturity, into a demand deposit (position 2), and transfers this demand deposit from the US bank to a Euro-bank. In the accounts of the US bank, the deposit liability to the resident now becomes a deposit liability to the Euro-bank (position 3), indicating that the latter now holds liquid claims on the US banking system amounting to $10. This is shown in the Euro-bank's balance sheet (position 1) as a $10 demand deposit claim on the US bank, the contra entry to which is a $10 time deposit liability to the US resident. The transfer of $10 by a US resident from a US to a Euro-bank has thus produced no change in total outstanding US liabilities, but has increased Euro-dollar assets and Euro-dollar liabilities by $10 each. If the Euro-bank now loans the $10 to a second US resident, the transaction will be recorded in the accounts of the Euro-bank as a $10 decrease in demand deposit claims on the US bank and a $10 increase in loans (non-deposit claims) to US residents (position 2), while in the accounts of the US bank the demand deposit liability to the Euro-bank will be converted into a demand deposit liability to the US resident (position 4).

The process of converting US residents' claims on the US banking system into Euro-dollar deposits and thence into Euro-dollar credits to other US residents has thus increased Euro-dollar assets and liabilities by $10 each but has generated no net changes in either the assets or liabilities of the US banking system.

Pyramided Euro-dollar Creation

Pyramided Euro-dollar creation arises when Euro-dollar deposits are intermediated by one or more banks before eventually being loaned to final use bank or non-bank borrowers. Unlike primary Euro-dollar creation, in which increases are recorded in Euro-dollar deposit liabilities and Euro-dollar deposit claims on the US, pyramided deposit creation results in increases in Euro-

Figure B-1

PRIMARY EURO-DOLLAR CREATION

US BANK

	LIABILITIES $		ASSETS $	
Position 1				
	Time deposit US resident	10	Various	10
Position 2				
	Time deposit US resident	-10	Various	10
	Demand deposit US resident	+10		
	NET CHANGE	0		0
Position 3				
	Demand deposit US resident	-10	Various	10
	Demand deposit Euro-bank	+10		
	NET CHANGE	0		0
Position 4				
	Demand deposit Euro-bank	-10	Various	10
	Demand deposit US resident	+10		
	NET CHANGE	0		0

EURO-BANK

	LIABILITIES $		ASSETS $	
Position 1				
	Time deposit US resident	+10	Demand deposit with US bank	+10
	NET CHANGE	+10		+10
Position 2				
	Time deposit US resident	10	Demand deposit with US bank	-10
			Loan to US resident	+10
	NET CHANGE	0		0

TOTAL NET CHANGES

	Liabilities	Assets
US Bank	---	---
Euro-bank	+10	+10
TOTAL PRIMARY EURO-DOLLAR CREATION	+10	+10

dollar deposit liabilities and Euro-dollar deposit claims on other Euro-banks.

The process of pyramided deposit creation is illustrated in figure B-2 (pp.136-7) and might commence with a US resident transfering to Euro-bank A $10 which, instead of being loaned to a second US resident and hence leaving the Euro-dollar market as in figure B-1, is deposited with a second Euro-bank (B). This results in the creation of a further $10 of Euro-dollar liabilities and $10 of Euro-dollar claims on other Euro-banks involving the redistribution of deposit claims on the US from Euro-bank A to Euro-bank B. If these $10 are then deposited with Euro-bank C which loans them to a Swiss firm, and if this firm uses the $10 to purchase goods from a US corporation which deposits them with a US bank, the Euro-dollar deposit will leave the market and the pyramiding process will cease.

The final result (shown at the foot of figure B-2) will be a zero net change in US reported assets and liabilities and the provision of $10 of final use credit. An additional $20 of assets and liabilities will also have been created, however, reflecting not the purchase of goods and services but merely the trail of statistical images as Euro-dollars are intermediated from banks A to C. It is this intermediation which is the essence of pyramided deposit creation.

Endogenous Euro-dollar Creation

Endogenous Euro-dollar creation arises when the market creates its own endogenous supply of final use credits, additional to those arising from the market's intermediation of deposits from the US to Europe. These credits increase international purchasing power and hence exert a real balance effect which may be contrasted with the statistical effect of pyramided deposits which do not change real economic variables.

The process of endogenous Euro-dollar creation is illustrated in figure B-3 (p.138) and commences at the point reached in figure B-2 when the Swiss firm pays the $10 Euro-dollar credit to the US corporation which, on this occasion, deposits the receipts with Euro-bank A rather than with the US bank. Bank A now incurs a $10 deposit liability to the US corporation and holds a $10 deposit claim on the US bank

Figure

PYRAMIDED EURO-

LIABILITIES $		ASSETS $	
	US BANK		
Position 1			
Time deposit US resident	-10	Various	10
Demand deposit Euro-bank A	+10		
NET CHANGE	0		0
Position 2			
Demand deposit Euro-bank A	-10	Various	10
Demand deposit Euro-bank B	+10		
NET CHANGE	0		0
Position 3			
Demand deposit Euro-bank B	-10	Various	10
Demand deposit Euro-bank C	+10		
NET CHANGE	0		0
Position 4			
Demand deposit Euro-bank C	-10	Various	10
Demand deposit Swiss firm	+10		
NET CHANGE	0		0
Position 5			
Demand deposit Swiss firm	-10	Various	10
Demand deposit US corporation	+10		
NET CHANGE	0		0

	TOTAL NET
US Bank	
Euro-bank A	
Euro-bank B	
Euro-bank C	
TOTAL PRIMARY EURO-DOLLAR CREATION	
TOTAL PYRAMIDED EURO-DOLLAR CREATION	

B-2

DOLLAR CREATION

LIABILITIES $		ASSETS $	
	EURO-BANK A		
Position 1			
Time deposit US resident	+10	Demand deposit with US Bank	+10
NET CHANGE	+10		+10
Position 2			
Time deposit US resident	10	Demand deposit with US Bank	-10
		Claim on Euro-bank B	+10
NET CHANGE	0		0
	EURO-BANK B		
Position 1			
Time deposit Euro-bank A	+10	Demand deposit with US Bank	+10
NET CHANGE	+10		+10
Position 2			
Time deposit Euro-bank A	10	Demand deposit with US Bank	-10
		Claim on Euro-bank C	+10
NET CHANGE	0		0
	EURO-BANK C		
Position 1			
Time deposit Euro-bank B	+10	Demand deposit with US Bank	+10
NET CHANGE	+10		+10
Position 2			
Time deposit Euro-bank B	10	Demand deposit with US Bank	-10
		Loan to Swiss firm	+10
NET CHANGE	0		0

CHANGES

LIABILITIES	ASSETS
---	---
+10	+10
+10	+10
+10	+10
+10	+10
+20	+20

Figure B-3
ENDOGENOUS EURO-DOLLAR CREATION

LIABILITIES $		ASSETS $	
	US BANK		
Position 1			
Demand deposit Euro-bank C	10	Various	10
Position 2			
Demand deposit Euro-bank C	-10	Various	10
Demand deposit Swiss firm	+10		
NET CHANGE	0		0
Position 3			
Demand deposit Swiss firm	-10	Various	10
Demand deposit US corporation	+10		
NET CHANGE	0		0
Position 4			
Demand deposit US corporation	-10	Various	10
Demand deposit Euro-bank A	+10		
NET CHANGE	0		0
	EURO-BANK A		
Position 1			
Time deposit US resident	10	Claim on Euro-bank B	10
Position 2			
Time deposit US corporation	+10	Demand deposit with US Bank	+10
NET CHANGE	+10		+10
	EURO-BANK B		
Position 1			
Time deposit Euro-bank A	10	Claim on Euro-bank C	10
	EURO-BANK C		
Position 1			
Time deposit Euro-bank B	10	Demand deposit with US Bank	10
Position 2			
Time deposit Euro-bank B	10	Demand deposit with US Bank	-10
		Loan to Swiss firm	+10
NET CHANGE	0		0

TOTAL NET CHANGES	Liabilities	Assets
US Bank	---	---
Euro-bank A	+20	+20
Euro-bank B	+10	+10
Euro-bank C	+10	+10
TOTAL PRIMARY EURO-DOLLAR CREATION	+10	+10
TOTAL PYRAMIDED EURO-DOLLAR CREATION	+20	+20
TOTAL ENDOGENOUS EURO-DOLLAR CREATION	+10	+10

(position 2). Two basic possibilities now arise:

Euro-bank A might lend the $10 to a second US corporation which utilises the funds for purely domestic purposes, in which case the deposit leaves the market and the process of endogenous deposit creation ceases. An additional $10 of international purchasing power (in effect a second final use credit) will thus have been created through endogenous deposit creation (primary and pyramided deposits -- assets plus liabilities -- will remain unchanged at $20 and $40 respectively).

Alternatively, Euro-bank A might redeposit the funds with Euro-bank B. This might arise, for example, if bank A specialised in deposit intermediation and eschewed the higher risks and returns of final use lending for the lower risks and returns of inter-bank intermediation, preferring to leave such lending to more risk-orientated banks. The final outcome would depend on whether the deposit was further intermediated or whether it was extended as a final use credit in which case either it might leave the market, thereby precluding further direct Euro-dollar activity, or it might be redeposited, thereby precipitating a further round of endogenous deposit creation.

Central Banks and Euro-dollar Creation

A special form of endogenous deposit creation, involving increases in both Euro-dollar deposits and international exchange reserves, arises when central banks deposit dollar reserves in the Euro-dollar market and the reserves, now in deposit form, are loaned to borrowers who use them to purchase domestic currencies either from those central banks with whom the reserves originated or from other central banks. If the central banks supplying the domestic currencies redeposit their newly acquired reserves in the Euro-dollar market, and if these reserves are again loaned out and used to finance further purchases of domestic currency, the result will be an increase in both Euro-dollar assets and liabilities as well as the statistical inflation of international exchange reserves.

The process of central bank deposit creation is illustrated in figure B-4 (p. 140) and commences with the transfer to the Euro-dollar market of a $10 US demand deposit which is loaned to

Figure B-4

OFFICIAL EURO-DOLLAR/RESERVE CREATION

Exchange rate: $1 = £1

EURO-BANKS

LIABILITIES $		ASSETS $	
Position 1			
Time deposit A	+10	Demand deposit with US Bank	+10
NET CHANGE	+10		+10
Position 2			
Time deposit A	10	Demand deposit with US Bank	-10
		Loan to B	+10
NET CHANGE	0		0
Position 3			
Time deposit A	10	Loan to B	10
Time deposit Central Bank	+10	Demand deposit with US Bank	+10
NET CHANGE	+10		+10
Position 4			
Time deposit A	10	Loan to B	10
Time deposit Central Bank	10	Demand deposit with US Bank	-10
		Loan to C	+10
NET CHANGE	0		0
Position 5			
Time deposit A	10	Loan to B	10
Time deposit Central Bank	10	Loan to C	10
Time deposit Central Bank	+10	Demand deposit with US Bank	+10
NET CHANGE	+10		+10

CENTRAL BANKS

LIABILITIES £		ASSETS (RESERVES) $	
Position 1			
Domestic Banks	+10	Demand deposit with US Bank	+10
NET CHANGE	+10		+10
Position 2			
Domestic Banks	10	Demand deposit with US Bank	-10
		Time deposit with Euro-banks	+10
NET CHANGE	0		0
Position 3			
Domestic Banks	10	Time deposit with Euro-banks	10
Domestic Banks	+10	Demand deposit with US Bank	+10
NET CHANGE	+10		+10
Position 4			
Domestic Banks	20	Time deposit with Euro-banks	10
		Demand deposit with US Bank	-10
		Time deposit with Euro-banks	+10
NET CHANGE	0		0

TOTAL NET CHANGES

	Liabilities	Assets
US BANK	---	---
EURO-BANKS	+30	+30
CENTRAL BANKS	+20	+20

borrower B. B then sells the deposit (in US demand deposit form) in the foreign exchange market where, because of exchange rate pressure and the need for official support measures, it is purchased by a central bank. This results in a $10 increase in official reserves and a £10 increase in domestic currency liabilities.[1] If the central bank now deposits these reserves in the Euro-dollar market which then loans the $10 to borrower C who uses them to effect further purchases of sterling from the central bank which again redeposits the reserves in the Euro-dollar market, the final position will be that domestic currency liabilities will have increased by £20 and central bank Euro-dollar deposits by $20. Euro-dollar liabilities, meanwhile, will have increased by $30 -- $20 vis-à-vis central banks and $10 vis-à-vis depositor A -- while Euro-dollar assets will also have increased by $30 -- $20 in loans to B and C and a $10 demand deposit claim on the US (total net changes outstanding at the end of the process are depicted at the foot of figure B-4).

The depositing of official reserves in the Euro-dollar market has thus increased Euro-dollar assets and liabilities and also inflated international exchange reserves. It is not this increase in Euro-dollar activity which poses a threat to international monetary stability, however, nor the increase in international reserves per se,[2] but rather the sustained selling of borrowed dollars. This will intensify exchange rate pressures even in the absence of conventional balance of payments considerations. Unlike more traditional forms of speculative activity, moreover, these flows are not constrained by any pre-existing level of financial resources, but only by the willingness of Euro-banks to continue extending credits to speculative borrowers and hence by the volume of reserves recycled to the market. In this way the dollar will have been subjected to heavy and sustained selling pressure, financed effectively by the central banks themselves. Through their redepositing actions, therefore, central banks will have provided the resources necessary to finance currency speculation and, in so doing, may have contributed to the realisation of anticipated exchange rate realignments.

EURO-DOLLAR CREATION IN PRACTICE

The practical creation of Euro-dollars has long been a contentious issue, focused principally on whether Euro-dollars are the result of concomitant or cumulative US payments deficits, whether they emanate from US gross capital outflows or whether they are, in fact, the product of endogenous deposit creation.

US Payments Deficits as a Source of Euro-dollars

US payments deficits constitute a prodigious potential source of Euro-dollar deposits, although a determinate causal relationship between deficits and the growth of the Euro-dollar market cannot be established, since deficits merely place dollar claims at the disposal of US non-residents who may or may not transfer these claims to the Euro-dollar market. Deficits are thus a sufficient but not necessary condition for deposit creation which is entirely consistent with balance of payments equilibria or even with balance of payments surpluses. The $26 billion growth of Euro-Deutsche Mark liabilities between 1971 and 1974, for example, corresponded to a $19 billion accumulated German payments surplus over the same period, thus refuting the alleged a priori link between payments deficits and Euro-currency growth.

The fallacy of a necessary link between US payments deficits and the growth of the Euro-dollar market is illustrated in figure B-5 (p.143). This compares changes in selected US payments positions with the growth of the net and gross Euro-dollar markets for the period 1958 - 1974, and shows convincingly that neither the cumulative US net liquidity deficit [3] nor the growth of US liquid liabilities to foreigners was sufficiently large to directly finance the growth of either market over this period. (This is not to deny the importance of deficit financing, however, for contained within aggregate net capital outflows are component flows such as increases in bank and non-bank reported short-term claims as well as errors and omissions, both of which may be expected to finance, at one stage or another, increases in off-shore dollar deposits).

A direct causal link between US payments deficits and the growth of Euro-dollar positions does not therefore exist.

Figure B-5

EURO-DOLLAR GROWTH [1] AND CHANGES IN SELECTED US PAYMENTS POSITIONS 1958 - 1974

($ billions)

	US Net Liquidity Balance	Increase in US Liquid Liabilities To Foreigners [2]	Increase in Net Euro-dollar Market	Increase in Gross Euro-dollar Market
1958-1964	- 21.6 [3]	+ 13.6	+ 9.0	+ 9.7
1965	- 2.5	+ 0.2	+ 2.5	+ 1.7
1966	- 2.2	+ 1.4	+ 3.0	+ 3.4
1967	- 4.7	+ 4.7	+ 3.0	+ 3.3
1968	- 1.6	+ 2.8	+ 7.5	+ 8.8
1969	- 6.1	+ 7.4	+ 12.5	+ 19.3
1970	- 3.9	+ 1.1	+ 8.5	+ 12.5
1971	- 22.0	+ 20.8	+ 8.0	+ 12.1
1972	- 13.8	+ 15.1	+ 17.0	+ 25.9
1973	- 7.7	+ 9.5	+ 26.0	+ 33.8
1974	- 19.0	+ 26.6	+ 36.0	+ 25.2
Total	-104.8	+103.2	+133.0	+155.7
TOTAL OUTSTANDING AT END 1974	--	119.0	133.0	155.7

Sources: Survey of Current Business, June 1969 and June 1975
Federal Reserve Bulletin, December 1967 and July 1975
Tables 2 and 15

1. A Euro-dollar base value of zero is assumed for December 1957
2. Excludes $0.6 billion arising from gold transactions with the IMF
3. Figures for 1958 and 1959 are based on liquidity balances

US Gross Capital Outflows as a Source of Euro-dollar Deposits

A second major potential source of Euro-dollar deposits is US gross capital outflows which also explain the apparent paradox of total Euro-dollar deposits exceeding aggregate US liabilities to foreigners without a necessary concomitant supply of endogenously created deposits.

Gross capital outflows are capable of financing increases in Euro-dollar deposits without corresponding increases in US payments deficits through the circular flow of dollar claims from the US to Europe. The transfer of demand deposits from the US to Europe, initiated either by US residents or non-residents, will create Euro-dollar deposits whose impact on the US balance of payments will depend on the form and ownership of the original dollar assets and the uses to which these deposits are put. Several flows are consistent with substantial Euro-dollar creation and a zero net change in the US balance of payments, the most prevalent of which arise from the simple transfer to Europe of a US non-resident claim on the US banking system and the maintenance of this claim in private circulation outside the US. This will increase both Euro-dollar assets and liabilities without any corresponding net change in either the US banking system or the US net liquidity balance. (If this deposit were subsequently used to finance US exports, the transaction would be recorded as a capital inflow which would generate a balance of payments surplus but which would still be consistent with the original creation of Euro-dollar deposits).

A significant volume of Euro-dollars may thus be created through US gross capital outflows independently of US payments deficits or net changes in US liquid liabilities to foreigners. Given the institutional mechanics of the Euro-dollar market and the substantial increase in net capital outflows (principally errors and omissions) recorded during periods of speculative activity, it seems most likely that US gross capital outflows have proved a significant source of Euro-dollar creation.

Endogenous Euro-dollar Creation

Whether or not the Euro-dollar market is capable

of significant endogenous deposit creation is a complex issue.

Studies which have attempted to respond to the question have been faced with serious statistical and conceptual difficulties. The most serious statistical problem has involved attempts to derive Euro-dollar reserve ratios to quantify the credit creating potential of primary deposit inflows. The problem has assumed a number of forms:

Firstly, it is unclear which, if any, is the most appropriate measure of Euro-dollar reserves to adopt. Demand deposit claims might initially be considered the most appropriate measure of a Euro-dollar reserve base but since, in the latter half of the sixties, Euro-banks extended a significant volume of non-deposit claims to their US head offices and since these claims could be readily recalled in exigencies, it might also be considered appropriate to include these claims in the market's reserve base.

Secondly, the acceptance of head office non-deposit claims as reserves might also be extended to embrace less liquid short-term claims on the US such as CDs since, for individual banks at least, such claims are readily convertible into cash (demand deposits).

Thirdly, regardless of the reserve measure adopted, it is difficult to distinguish between reserves maintained for Euro-dollar and non-Euro-dollar uses and, to a lesser extent, between reserves maintained by Euro- and non-Euro-banks.

Finally, it is by no means apparent which measure of the Euro-dollar market should be adopted, since the net measure might prove more appropriate for an evaluation of the economic consequences of primary inflows whilst the gross measure might prove more appropriate for estimating the multiplicative potential of these inflows.

Several different criteria may thus be employed in the computation of Euro-dollar reserve ratios and, by extension, deposit multipliers. A selection of these ratios is illustrated in figure B-6 (p. 146) which shows that, depending on the criteria adopted, reserve ratios range from 5% for demand deposit liabilities to foreign commercial banks reported by New York City banks to 40% for US banks' total short-term liabilities to foreign commercial banks. These values emphasise the range of potential market reserve ratios compared to the relatively unified ratios of

Figure B-6

EURO-DOLLAR RESERVE RATIOS CALCULATED ON THE BASIS OF SELECTED RESERVE
1964 - 1974

(%)

	r_1 as % of		r_2 as % of		$r_2 + r_3$ as % of		r_4 as % of		
	Net Mkt	Gross Mkt	Net Mkt	Gross Mkt	Net Mkt	Gross Mkt	Net Mkt	Gross Mkt	Ne
	3.0	2.8	4.4	4.1	17.5	16.2	29.4	27.3	
	2.5	2.5	3.9	3.9	15.6	15.7	22.6	22.8	
	2.6	2.6	3.8	3.8	31.7	31.0	16.8	16.4	
	3.3	3.1	4.5	4.4	28.8	27.8	19.3	18.6	
	3.3	2.7	4.4	4.1	28.6	26.6	19.8	16.6	
	2.6	2.1	3.9	3.2	40.3	32.7	17.4	14.1	
	2.2	1.8	3.0	2.4	18.8	14.7	14.0	11.0	
	1.8	1.3	2.6	2.0	6.9	5.2	8.3	6.3	
	2.6	1.9	3.5	2.6	6.5	4.8	12.8	9.4	
	2.9	2.2	3.8	2.8	5.7	4.3	12.7	9.4	
	2.9	2.4	3.8	3.3	7.2	6.1	16.8	14.4	
e	2.7	2.3	3.8	3.3	18.9	16.8	17.3	15.1	

emand deposit liabilities to foreign commercial banks reported by large New York City banks
emand deposit liabilities to foreign commercial banks reported by large US banks
iabilities of US banks to their foreign branches
otal short-term liabilities to foreign commercial banks reported by US banks exclusive of r_3
otal short-term liabilities to foreign commercial banks reported by US banks

Sources: BIS Annual Report,
<u>US Treasury Bullet</u>
<u>Federal Reserve Bu</u>

i) A Euro-dollar base value of zero is assumed for 1957
i) Data refer to commercial banks in all non-US financial centres

domestic banking systems and hence the range of market deposit multipliers and attendant potential for endogenous deposit creation.

The most serious conceptual shortcoming associated with studies of credit creation has been the assumption of a quantifiable determinate relationship between market reserve ratios and total Euro-dollar positions. This has invited direct comparisons between the Euro-dollar market and conventional domestic banking systems with the consequent adoption of the reciprocal of the market's reserve ratio as a statistical measure of the Euro-dollar market's deposit multiplier. Such reasoning is fallacious, however, for any given reserve ratio is consistent with a redeposit ratio of 0% to 100%. It is consequently erroneous to derive a deposit multiplier of twenty or more on the basis of a reserve ratio of 5% or less for, unlike in a closed domestic banking system where the reciprocal of the reserve ratio is indicative of deposit creating potential, the Euro-dollar market's reserve ratio is rendered an unreliable and singularly inappropriate tool for assessing Euro-dollar deposit creating potential by the existence of a potentially low redeposit (high leakages) ratio -- a failing of particular relevance to the late sixties when US banks' Euro-dollar borrowing reduced alternative deposit usage (low redeposit ratio) and attendant scope for endogenous deposit creation.

In the light of these shortcomings, it is instructive to consider how market studies have attempted to reconcile these difficulties and why derived credit/deposit multipliers have ranged from zero [4] to 18.45. [5]

One of the earlier estimates of the market's endogenous deposit creating capacity was published in 1971 by G. Carli, [6] who derived an implicit multiplier on the basis of the ratio of Euro-banks' claims on the US to net market positions. The resultant multiplier ranged from 2.3 (1969) to 5.5 (1965), on which basis Carli ventured that:

> Using more sophisticated analytical methods it appears that this money multiplier could even climb to a ratio

> of seven times liquid reserves held by Eurobanks if (as is now taking place) there were a weakening in the needs (or the simple holdings) of dollars held by US banks.

Carli assumed, however, firstly that total Euro-banks' claims on the US constituted a reliable measure of Euro-dollar reserves and secondly, and more importantly, that a 100% redeposit ratio was applicable. Both his estimates and his claim, therefore, are subject to some analytical reservations.

In the same publication,[7] M. Fratianni and P. Savona estimated, using US banks' indebtedness to their foreign branches as a proxy of the stock of Euro-banks' reserve assets, that the Euro-dollar market was creating $7 of deposits for each dollar of International Monetary Base in its possession in 1964, but that by the end of 1969 US banks' Euro-dollar borrowings had reduced this figure to $3. Whilst acknowledging that these values would change as the "statistical endowment improved", the authors sought, in the meantime, to confirm the general dimension of their estimates with the cash-deposit ratios reported by the foreign branches of US banks. Since the reciprocal of these ratios for the years 1968 and 1969 corresponded closely with the multiplier estimates which the authors had derived using their first approach, Fratianni and Savona concluded that the general dimension of their multiplier values had been confirmed. Their estimates, like Carli's, suffered firstly from a computational disregard of the market's redeposit ratio and secondly, from the use of US banks' foreign branches' cash-deposit ratios as a proxy of the market's reserve ratio which, because branches' cash assets include claims on other Euro-banks, served to overstate the volume of claims acting as reserves for the market as a whole.[8]

In a subsequent study published in 1972,[9] J.H. Makin estimated that the long-run value of the Euro-dollar market's deposit multiplier was 18.45 for the period 1964 - 1970, and the consensus of these studies was no better illustrated than in the following year, when B.E. Lee[10] estimated that for the period 1963 - 1969 (a period almost identical to that examined by Makin), the market's deposit multiplier ranged from a low of 1.3

in 1963 to a high of 1.9 in 1969! One of the principal causes of the marked disparity between these results was that in neither study was provision made for a variable leakages ratio, although Lee implicitly recognised this fact when, commenting on his multiplier values, he stated that:

> It may seem surprising that a system with no minimal reserve requirements would exhibit so small a multiplier. It does, of course, because the leakages from the system are indeed massive. Only a relatively small portion of total Euro-dollar loans ever return to Euro-banks as secondary deposits. A portion does indeed return, however, and that portion is growing.[11]

Yet it was not until 1974 that the existence of a potentially low redeposit ratio was quantitatively recognised, when J. Hewson and E. Sakakibara noted that:

> It is somewhat surprising that few of the participants in this debate have objected to the fixed-coefficient version of the money-multiplier model as a conceptual framework for discussion of the Euro-dollar deposit multiplier.[12]

Developing their argument further, they remarked that:

> ...these criticisms seem to have centered on the fixed leakages assumptions of the model, which preclude explicit portfolio choice on the part of Euro-banks and the non-Euro-bank public.,[13]

and that:

> ...while the multiplier model may have plausibility as a simple approximation to the money supply process in a regulated domestic system, it is inappropriate for an unregulated competitive situation such as that of the Euro-dollar market.[14]

Hewson and Sakakibara then proceeded to derive estimates of the market's deposit multiplier using deposit-loan variables based on monthly dollar positions reported by the Bank of England. Since these positions were not disaggregated to eliminate non-primary flows, the authors' result of a deposit multiplier ranging from zero to unity was not altogether surprising.

A further study of consequence to the disparities of multiplier values was that published by J.P. Owens in 1974.[15] After observing that Euro-dollar reserve ratios had been an unimportant factor in the market's credit creating potential, Owens reduced the entire issue to the question of whether or not a significant redeposit ratio existed. Proceeding to reject the existence of such a ratio arising from new saving generated by Euro-dollar activity, he estimated that on the basis of central bank redepositing the market's multiplier ranged from 1.04 to 1.17 between 1965 and 1967. [16] Summarising the entire question of a Euro-dollar multiplier, Owens concluded that:

> ...neither side of the debate is correct. The euro-dollar system is capable of having an indigenous multiplier of greater than one; but during our period we saw that this potential was not realised. Between 1965 and 1969 we can say that any final-use credit extended by the market was almost entirely the result of the ability of the euro-banks to attract new funds and not of any indigenous credit multiplier.[17]

Finally, a study which attempted to place both endogenous deposit creation and the wider role of the Euro-dollar market in a broader portfolio/liquidity context was published in 1976 by J. Niehans and J. Hewson,[18] who ventured:

> ...that the bank that accepts monetary liabilities to buy nonmonetary assets is an inappropriate paradigm for the Euro-dollar market, and that this market is more fruitfully interpreted in terms of an antithetical paradigm, at once older and newer, of a bank borrowing and lending funds of approximately the same "moneyness" in a perfect market. Once this is recognized,

the Eurodollar market in turn becomes the paradigm for an important basic function of financial intermediaries which the dominant model tends to suppress, namely, the function of efficient distributors of funds.

It is evident from the marked disparities to have emerged from market studies that considerable shortcomings exist in both the statistical and conceptual treatment of endogenous Euro-dollar creation. On the one hand it is statistically impossible to disaggregate and quantify primary market inflows, so that even if endogenous multiplier estimates were obtainable, they would prove of limited practical application. On the other hand, failure to take into account the market's redeposit ratio resulting from high deposit attrition invalidates the expectation that the Euro-dollar market will exhibit flow pattern characteristics more appropriately attributable to domestic banking systems operating within "closed" frameworks. In many ways, therefore, the whole multiplier debate has been conducted on spurious grounds. Those analysts who have resorted to orthodox criteria in their computation of Euro-dollar multipliers have derived results of limited application, whilst those who have recognised the shortcomings of fixed coefficient leakages ratios have been so constrained by data insufficiencies that their results, too, must be treated with circumspection.

Since the question of an endogenous Euro-dollar multiplier hinges on a computationally indeterminate redeposit ratio, it is difficult to escape the conclusion that exact quantification of a Euro-dollar deposit multiplier and hence, of the market's endogenous deposit creating capacity, is rendered all but impossible by the insuperable constraints of data insufficiencies.

NOTES

1. It may be assumed for ease of exposition that the authorities make no attempt to neutralise the expansionary impact of this currency inflow and that dollars are sold for sterling at an exchange rate of $1 = £1.

2. If increases in reserve holdings trigger policy changes designed to correct exchange "imbalances", the subsequent shock to underlying equilibrium may be such as to precipitate a situation of genuine disequilibrium, in which case the growth of reserves would, of itself, have been inherently destabilising.

3. The net liquidity balance is the most appropriate measure to employ since it was used extensively in US balance of payments data in the sixties and early seventies.

4. J. Hewson and E. Sakakibara: "The Euro-Dollar Deposit Multiplier: A Portfolio Approach", IMF Staff Papers, July 1974, p.326.

5. J.H. Makin: "Demand and Supply Functions for Stocks of Euro-Dollar Deposits: An Empirical Study", The Review of Economics and Statistics, November 1972, p.389.

6. G. Carli: "Eurodollars: A Paper Pyramid", Banca Nazionale del Lavoro Quarterly Review no. 97 (June 1971), p.95.

7. M. Fratianni and P. Savona: "Eurodollar Creation: Comments on Professor Machlup's Propositions and Developments" Banca Nazionale del Lavoro Quarterly Review no. 97 (June 1971), p.118.

8. The margin of error present in Fratianni and Savona's estimates did not escape the attention of H. Mayer, who remarked that: "...after the large repayments by US banks in 1970-71 their [Fratianni and Savona's] multiplier would now even have to exceed the figure given for 1963. This would imply that the endogenous multiplier potential of the Euro-dollar market is larger than that of the US commercial banking system!" H. Mayer: "Multiplier Effects and Credit Creation in the Euro-dollar Market", Banca Nazionale del Lavoro Quarterly Review no. 98 (September 1971), p.239.

9. J.H. Makin: art.cit. p.389.

10. B.E. Lee: "The Euro-Dollar Multiplier", Journal of Finance, September 1973, p.867.

11. Ibid. p.871.

12. J. Hewson and E. Sakakibara: art.cit. p.308.

13. *Ibid.* p.309.

14. *Ibid.*

15. J.P. Owens: *Growth of the Euro-Dollar Market*, (University of Wales Press, Bangor Occasional Papers in Economics no.4, 1974).

16. *Ibid.* p.147.

17. *Ibid.* p.151.

18. J. Niehans and J. Hewson: "The Eurodollar Market and Monetary Theory", *Journal of Money, Credit and Banking* vol. VIII no.1 (February 1976), p.2.

Table 1

DOLLAR-DENOMINATED EXTERNAL LIABILITIES AND CLAIMS OF UK BANKS 1957 - 1974

($ millions and %)

	LIABILITIES TO							CLAIMS ON						
	US	%	Western Europe	%	Other	%	Total	US	%	Western Europe	%	Other	%	Total
1957	--	--	---	--	---	--	157	--	--	---	--	---	--	---
1958	--	--	---	--	---	--	308	--	--	---	--	---	--	---
1959	--	--	---	--	---	--	678	--	--	---	--	---	--	---
1960	--	--	---	--	---	--	1579	--	--	---	--	---	--	---
1961	--	--	---	--	---	--	1870	--	--	---	--	---	--	---
1962	288	12	1257	51	930	38	2475	904	40	941	42	403	18	2248
1963	384	13	1456	49	1162	39	3002	795	28	1453	51	619	22	2867
1964	535	12	2005	46	1840	42	4379	1210	33	1680	46	784	21	3674
1965	529	10	2853	54	1918	36	5300	1596	35	1795	39	1156	25	4547
1966	952	12	4211	55	2472	32	7636	3466	47	2349	32	1495	20	7311
1967	1385	14	5191	54	3115	32	9691	4068	44	2539	28	2602	28	9209
1968	2568	17	8186	53	4615	30	15370	7248	48	3698	25	4042	27	14988
1969	2894	11	13764	53	9089	35	25747	13301	53	6324	25	5609	22	25234
1970	2928	9	17592	56	10886	35	31406	9758	33	10531	36	8964	31	29254
1971	3218	9	20254	55	13456	36	36928	5099	15	14149	41	14897	44	34145
1972	3400	7	25205	52	19623	41	48228	5215	11	18087	40	22302	49	45605
1973	4642	7	35861	52	28667	41	69171	6696	10	24764	38	34002	52	65462
1974	7051	8	---	--	---	--	88973	9964	12	---	--	---	--	82688

Source: Bank of England Quarterly Bulletin, various issues

Table 2
ESTIMATED NET SIZE OF THE EURO-DOLLAR MARKET
1964 - 1974

($ billions)

	1964	1965	1966	1967	1968	1969	1970	1971	1972
OF FUNDS									
	2.6	4.4	5.6	5.7	8.0	8.5	11.3	--	--
ks	1.8	2.2	2.8	3.9	5.2	9.8	9.7	--	--
NSIDE AREA	4.4	6.6	8.4	9.6	13.2	18.3	21.0	--	--
	0.6	0.7	1.1	1.7	3.2	3.8	4.2	--	--
World	4.0	4.2	5.0	6.2	8.6	15.4	20.8	--	--
UTSIDE AREA	4.6	4.9	6.1	7.9	11.8	19.2	25.0	--	--
	9.0	11.5	14.5	17.5	25.0	37.5	46.0	54.0	71.0
FUNDS									
	2.7	3.0	2.6	2.8	3.3	6.0	7.3	--	--
ks	2.3	3.3	3.7	4.1	4.7	5.6	10.1	--	--
NSIDE AREA	5.0	6.3	6.3	6.9	7.9	11.6	17.4	--	--
	1.8	2.0	4.4	5.2	9.5	16.5	12.7	--	--
World	2.2	3.2	3.8	5.4	7.6	9.4	15.9	--	--
UTSIDE AREA	4.0	5.2	8.2	10.6	17.1	25.9	28.6	--	--
	9.0	11.5	14.5	17.5	25.0	37.5	46.0	54.0	71.0

BIS Annual Report, various issues

Table 3

'EREST RATES ON THREE-MONTH LONDON EURO-DOLLAR DEPOSITS AND US TREASURY B

1960 - 1974

(% p.a.)

1960	1961	1962	1963	1964	1965	1966	1967	1968	1969	1970	1971	1972	
4.76	3.75	3.44	3.38	4.96	4.50	5.38	5.69	5.44	7.69	9.59	5.88	5.06	[illegible]
4.66	3.63	3.50	3.38	4.06	4.56	5.41	5.69	5.66	8.50	9.44	5.34	4.97	[illegible]
4.34	3.69	3.66	3.63	4.31	4.94	5.81	5.38	6.38	8.53	8.63	5.38	5.53	[illegible]
4.31	3.66	3.41	3.69	4.13	4.81	5.78	4.69	6.66	8.56	8.69	6.25	5.00	[illegible]
4.16	3.66	3.81	3.81	4.19	5.19	5.84	5.06	7.16	10.56	9.19	7.63	4.63	[illegible]
4.13	3.50	3.75	3.84	4.38	4.88	6.13	5.38	6.88	10.56	9.06	6.50	5.31	[illegible]
3.88	3.38	3.84	4.00	4.25	4.69	6.44	5.06	6.31	10.44	8.50	6.72	5.66	1
3.63	3.31	3.78	4.00	4.25	4.50	6.84	5.06	6.16	11.31	8.00	9.25	5.50	1
3.88	3.38	3.94	4.13	4.19	4.50	7.06	5.78	6.25	11.25	8.50	7.63	5.94	1
4.06	3.44	4.13	4.13	4.50	5.06	7.06	5.69	6.59	10.00	7.72	5.06	6.03	[illegible]
4.22	3.63	4.00	4.19	5.00	5.19	7.19	7.00	6.94	11.00	7.25	5.50	6.00	1
4.25	3.88	3.94	4.56	4.50	5.31	6.56	6.31	7.13	10.06	6.56	5.75	5.91	1
4.19	3.58	3.76	3.89	4.39	4.84	6.29	5.57	6.46	9.87	8.43	6.57	5.47	[illegible]
2.93	2.38	2.78	3.16	3.55	3.95	4.88	4.32	5.34	6.68	6.46	4.35	4.07	[illegible]

nancial Statistics, various issues

deral Reserve Bulletin, various issues

nk of England Quarterly Bulletin, various issues

Table 4

IDENTIFIED OFFICIAL HOLDINGS OF EURO-DOLLARS
1964 - 1974

($ billions)

	1964	1965	1966	1967	1968	1969	1970	1971	197
ial countries	1.0	0.9	1.4	1.2	2.3	2.2	5.1	3.7	6.
il-exporting countries					0.4	0.8	1.6	3.0	4.
	0.5	0.6	0.6	1.0					
					1.1	1.9	3.7	4.5	9.
	1.5	1.5	2.0	2.2	3.8	4.9	10.4	11.2	19.

IMF Annual Report, various issues

Table 5

US BANKS' LIABILITIES TO FOREIGN BRANCHES
1964 - 1974

($ millions)

h	1964	1965	1966	1967	1968	1969	1970	1971	1972	19
	1040	1358	1688	3653	4259	8545	13644	6125	1986	23
	1077	1592	1902	3396	4530	8822	12862	5131	1742	15
	1046	1431	1879	3412	4920	9621	12066	4055	2085	19
	1146	1433	1909	3047	5020	9399	12608	2511	2426	16
	1132	1432	2003	2776	5872	9868	12129	2191	2080	19
	917	1436	1951	3166	6202	13269	12089	2661	2279	23
	1008	1572	2786	3660	6126	14434	10360	2619	1524	25
	1166	1792	3134	3976	7004	14658	10856	2036	1760	22
	1166	1611	3472	4059	7104	14338	10253	2970	2243	19
	1198	1719	3671	4322	7041	14307	9274	3649	2239	18
	1380	1697	3786	4206	7170	14499	8003	3341	1824	28
	1183	1345	4036	4241	6948	13660	7248	2310	2113	18

al Reserve Bulletin, various issues

Table 6

SELECTED CENTRAL BANK DISCOUNT RATES
December 1968 – December 1969

(% p.a.)

	Dec	Jan	Feb	Mar	Apr	May	June	July	Aug	Sept	Oct
m	4.50	4.50	4.50	5.00	5.50	6.00	6.00	7.00	7.00	7.50	7.[illegible]
	6.50	6.50	6.50	7.00	7.00	7.00	7.50	8.00	8.00	8.00	8.[illegible]
k	6.00	6.00	6.00	7.00	7.00	9.00	9.00	9.00	9.00	9.00	9.[illegible]
	6.00	6.00	6.00	6.00	6.00	6.00	7.00	7.00	7.00	7.00	8.[illegible]
y	3.00	3.00	3.00	3.00	4.00	4.00	5.00	5.00	5.00	5.00	6.[illegible]
	3.50	3.50	3.50	3.50	3.50	3.50	3.50	3.50	4.00	4.00	4.[illegible]
rland	3.00	3.00	3.00	3.00	3.00	3.00	3.00	3.00	3.00	3.75	3.[illegible]
	7.00	7.00	8.00	8.00	8.00	8.00	8.00	8.00	8.00	8.00	8.[illegible]

International Financial Statistics, various issues

Table 7 (i)

EXTERNAL LIABILITIES OF REPORTING EUROPEAN BANKS IN DOLLARS AND OTHER EUROPEAN CURRENCIES[1] 1966 - 1974

($ millions)

		DOLLARS				OTHER CURRENCIES			
		Vis-à-vis			Total	Vis-à-vis			Total
		Banks	Non-banks	Non-Bank Res.[3]		Banks	Non-banks	Non-Bank Res.[3]	
1966	Q4	10640	4130		14770	3180	510		3690
1967	Q2	10840	4090		14930	3780	510		4290
	Q4	13440	4680		18120	3860	470		4330
1968	Q2	15990	6390		22380	5100	700		5800
	Q4	20630	6240		26870	5850	1040		6890
1969	Q1	22280	7600		29880	6740	930		7670
	Q2	29270	8690		37960	8130	1320		9450
	Q3	31580	9960		41540	8900	1340		10240
	Q4	35740	10460		46200	9320	1320		10640
1970	Q1	34950	11100		46050	10040	1370		11410
	Q2	38440	11000		49440	11430	1660		13090
	Q3	39460	10770		50230	12880	2310		15190
	Q4	47460	11240		58700	14140	2450		16590
1971	Q1	48480	11120		59600	15470	2530		18000
	Q2	51020	10910		61930	17290	3110		20400
	Q3[2]	53050	9380		62430	19950	2700		22650
	Q4	60770	9980	2450	70750	24230	2750	1150	26980
1972	Q1	63050	10050		73100	25730	2760		28490
	Q2	64590	11340		75930	27720	3670		31390
	Q3	70430	11700		82130	30300	3940		34240
	Q4	84920	11810	3260	96730	31580	3620	1720	35200
1973	Q1	89130	12940		102070	37120	4740		41860
	Q2	86430	13680		100110	48060	5560		53620
	Q3	95260	14480		109740	54250	5810		60060
	Q4	114100	16370	5020	130470	55350	5610	2560	60960
1974	Q1	125320	18660		143980	58880	6310		65190
	Q2	132020	19660		151680	60530	7310		67840
	Q3	127000	19930		146930	52770	7410		60180
	Q4[4]	132580	23110	8560	155690	55940	8050	3780	63990

Source: <u>BIS Annual Report</u>, various issues

1. Deutsche Marks, Swiss francs, sterling, French francs, guilders and lire.
2. Break in series - figures exclude Swiss trustee funds.
3. Excludes Germany. These columns are memorandum items and are not included in totals.
4. Break in series. Figures exclude currency positions of the BIS, but include certain long-term positions previously excluded.

Table 7 (ii)

EXTERNAL ASSETS OF REPORTING EUROPEAN BANKS IN DOLLARS AND OTHER EUROPEAN CURRENCIES[1] 1966 - 1974

($ millions)

	DOLLARS Vis-à-vis			Total	OTHER CURRENCIES Vis-à-vis			Total
	Banks	Non-banks	Non-Bank Res.[3]		Banks	Non-banks	Non-Bank Res.[3]	
1966 Q4	13970	2100		16070	3490	690		4180
1967 Q2	13930	2650		16580	4060	810		4870
Q4	16460	3430		19890	4110	850		4960
1968 Q2	21240	4320		25560	4550	1340		5890
Q4	25280	5150		30430	5900	1500		7400
1969 Q1	28420	5230		33650	5760	1670		7430
Q2	36340	5940		42280	7150	2030		9180
Q3	38710	6110		44820	8300	2520		10820
Q4	41540	6090		47630	8540	2160		10700
1970 Q1	40210	6760		46970	9300	2470		11770
Q2	43470	8560		52030	10120	2980		13100
Q3	43040	9890		52930	11530	3940		15470
Q4	48520	11850		60370	13210	4670		17880
1971 Q1	49080	13380		62460	13630	5590		19220
Q2	51040	14040		65080	14790	5960		20750
Q3[2]	49610	13830		63440	17560	6350		23910
Q4	57140	14360	5850	71500	21880	6750	1770	28630
1972 Q1	60100	13650		73750	22730	6770		29500
Q2	62160	15030		77190	24500	7410		31910
Q3	67790	16290		84080	25260	8350		33610
Q4	79660	18340	5120	98000	25840	8000	3530	33840
1973 Q1	78650	19450		98100	33870	9230		43100
Q2	80980	20290		101270	40620	10710		51330
Q3	90730	21150		111880	43320	12420		55740
Q4	109890	23870	8830	133760	42840	12000	5150	54840
1974 Q1	117390	28710		146100	44440	14090		58530
Q2	122870	31300		154170	44880	14790		59670
Q3	117670	31300		148970	37500	15250		52750
Q4[4]	121100	34570	16430	155670	40550	17900	6330	58450

Source: BIS Annual Report, various issues

1,2,3,4: See table 7 (i).

Table 7 (iii)

EXTERNAL NET POSITIONS OF REPORTING EUROPEAN BANKS IN DOLLARS AND OTHER EUROPEAN CURRENCIES[1] 1966 - 1974

($ millions)

	DOLLARS				OTHER CURRENCIES			
	Vis-à-vis			Total	Vis-à-vis			Total
	Banks	Non-banks			Banks	Non-banks		
1966 Q4	+ 3330	- 2030		+1300	+ 310	+ 180		+ 490
1967 Q2	+ 3090	- 1440		+1650	+ 280	+ 300		+ 580
Q4	+ 3020	- 1250		+1770	+ 250	+ 380		+ 630
1968 Q2	+ 5250	- 2070		+3180	- 550	+ 640		+ 90
Q4	+ 4650	- 1090		+3560	+ 50	+ 460		+ 510
1969 Q1	+ 6140	- 2370		+3770	- 980	+ 740		- 240
Q2	+ 7070	- 2750		+4320	- 980	+ 710		- 270
Q3	+ 7130	- 3850		+3280	- 600	+1180		+ 580
Q4	+ 5800	- 4370		+1430	- 780	+ 840		+ 60
1970 Q1	+ 5260	- 4340		+ 920	- 740	+1100		+ 360
Q2	+ 5030	- 2440		+2590	- 1310	+1320		+ 10
Q3	+ 3580	- 880		+2700	- 1350	+1630		+ 280
Q4	+ 1060	+ 610		+1670	+ 2220	+1290		+3510
1971 Q1	+ 600	+ 2260	Non-[3]	+2860	- 1840	+3060	Non-[3]	+1220
Q2	+ 20	+ 3130	Bank	+3150	- 2500	+2850	Bank	+ 350
Q3[2]	- 3440	+ 4450	Res.	+1010	- 2390	+3650	Res.	+1260
Q4	- 3630	+ 4380	+3400	+ 750	- 2350	+4000	+ 620	+1650
1972 Q1	- 2950	+ 3600		+ 650	- 3000	+4010		+1010
Q2	- 2430	+ 3690		+1260	- 3220	+3740		+ 520
Q3	- 2640	+ 4590		+1950	- 5040	+4410		- 630
Q4	- 5260	+ 6530	+1860	+1270	- 5740	+4380	+1810	-1360
1973 Q1	-10480	+ 6510		-3970	- 3250	+4490		+1240
Q2	- 5450	+ 6610		+1160	- 7440	+5150		-2290
Q3	- 4530	+ 6670		+2140	-10930	+6610		-4320
Q4	- 4210	+ 7500	+3810	+3290	-12510	+6390	+2590	-6120
1974 Q1	- 7930	+10050		+2120	-14440	+7780		-6660
Q2	- 9150	+11640		+2490	-15650	+7480		-8170
Q3	- 9330	+11370		+2040	-15270	+7840		-7430
Q4[4]	-11480	+11460	+7870	- 20	-15390	+9850	+2550	-5540

Source: Tables 7 (i) and 7 (ii)

1,2,3,4: See table 7 (i).

Table 8

HANGES IN DOLLAR-DENOMINATED ASSETS AND LIABILITIES OF US BANKS' FOREIGN
1971 - 1973

($ millions)

CLAIMS ON						LIABILITIES T			
US	Foreign Banks	Official Instit-utions	Foreign Non-Banks	Other	Total	US	Foreign Banks	Official Instit-utions	Foreign Non-Banks
- 854	- 399	+ 8	+ 38	+ 890	- 316	- 57	+ 43	+ 81	-361
- 889	- 127	+ 53	+420	+ 165	- 379	-157	- 761	+388	+236
-1083	+1443	+ 30	+320	+ 411	+1121	+293	+ 657	+117	+ 45
-1704	+ 485	+ 77	+369	+1535	+ 762	-129	+ 587	+420	-182
- 663	+ 316	+ 24	+595	+ 56	+ 328	+298	+ 228	-324	+ 18
+ 455	+1061	+ 33	+ 49	- 19	+1578	-289	+1814	+185	+145
- 35	- 807	+127	- 41	+ 225	- 531	+469	- 778	-188	-245
- 712	+1870	+152	+ 80	- 510	+ 879	+182	+ 603	- 41	+428
+ 932	+1208	+ 9	+225	-1509	+ 866	-302	+1132	+ 33	-205
+ 793	- 69	+ 32	+208	-1106	- 142	- 88	- 245	+ 95	+115
- 232	+ 730	+ 3	+ 69	- 9	+ 560	- 26	+ 650	+159	+ 8
- 827	+1539	- 46	+454	- 67	+1052	+151	+1110	-229	+ 54
- 471	- 528	- 42	-326	+ 51	-1315	-122	-1153	+293	+361
- 206	+1010	- 1	+190	+ 54	+1048	+188	+1026	+ 57	- 63
+ 436	+2182	+ 22	+491	- 51	+3078	- 98	+2783	+174	+176
+ 262	-1956	+ 38	- 21	+ 37	-1640	- 53	-1964	+245	-142
- 169	+ 677	+ 55	+ 33	- 15	+ 582	-178	+ 837	- 32	+ 73
+ 192	+2597	- 22	+205	- 2	+2970	+260	+2833	+486	+ 68

- 774	+ 279	+ 70	+505	+ 49	+ 129	+ 83	- 811	+121	+183	+
+ 452	+1111	+ 79	+472	+ 28	+2141	+ 46	+1249	+475	+106	+
+ 404	+ 51	+ 41	- 73	+ 151	+ 574	- 7	+ 424	+ 79	+121	+
+ 2	+ 863	- 19	+516	- 118	+1246	- 4	+ 536	+236	+453	+
- 496	+ 611	- 2	+491	+ 32	+ 636	- 36	+ 500	+167	+101	+
+ 300	+3428	+ 45	+632	+ 24	+4427	+351	+3449	+179	+102	+
+ 119	- 133	- 65	+257	- 40	+ 138	-109	- 798	+767	+333	-
- 607	+3522	+ 34	+307	+ 114	+3371	+471	+3140	+128	+400	+
+ 3	+ 627	+ 27	+407	+ 114	+1178	+147	+1093	- 37	+289	+
- 399	-1082	- 16	+217	+ 50	-1230	- 51	-1239	- 28	-255	+
+ 341	- 699	+ 32	+667	+ 163	+ 504	+443	+ 446	-369	- 44	+
+ 672	+2529	- 11	+497	+ 138	+3824	+ 30	+3171	- 20	- 7	+

al *Reserve Bulletin*, various issues

Table 9

PUBLICLY-ANNOUNCED MEDIUM-TERM FOREIGN CURRENCY CREDIT FACILITIES BY DOMICILE OF BORROWER 1970 - 1974

($ billions and %)

Domicile of Borrower	1970	1971	1972	1973	1974
Developed countries	4.2	2.6	4.1	13.8	20.7
%	89	65	60	63	71
Less-developed countries (Non-OPEC)	0.3	0.9	1.5	4.5	6.3
%	6	23	22	21	21
Less-developed countries (OPEC)	0.1	0.3	0.9	2.8	1.1
%	2	8	13	13	4
Socialist countries	*	0.1	0.3	0.8	1.2
%	*	2	4	4	4
TOTAL	4.7	4.0	6.8	21.9	29.3

* Negligible

Source: World Financial Markets, various issues

Table 10

PUBLICLY-ANNOUNCED MEDIUM-TERM FOREIGN CURRENCY CREDIT FACILITIES BY MATURITY DISTRIBUTION 1974

(%)

Maturity	Q 1	Q 2	Q 3	Q 4	Year
Under 7 years	15.3	7.2	37.2	35.8	18.3
7 - under 10 years	53.8	85.0	44.5	48.1	65.4
10 years and over	24.1	4.4	10.0	10.0	10.8
Unknown	6.8	3.4	8.3	6.1	5.4
TOTAL	100.0	100.0	100.0	100.0	100.0

Source: IMF Survey, May 1975

Table 11

PUBLICLY-ANNOUNCED MEDIUM-TERM FOREIGN CURRENCY CREDIT FACILITIES BY CATEGORY OF BORROWER 1974

($ millions and %)

Category of Borrower	Q_1	Q_2	Q_3	Q_4	Year
Industrial Countries					
Government and Public Financial Institutions	1661	6318	595	17	8591
%	24	51	13	1	32
Public Utilities	813	900	510	332	2555
%	12	7	11	9	9
Private Financial Institutions	251	243	37	53	584
%	4	2	1	2	2
Other	1175	1360	1293	1080	4908
%	17	11	29	30	18
TOTAL	3900	8821	2435	1482	16638
%	57	71	54	42	61
Developing Countries					
Government and Public Financial Institutions	1876	1536	614	342	4368
%	27	12	14	9	16
Public Utilities	204	352	152	429	1137
%	3	3	3	12	4
Private Financial Institutions	47	85	12	26	170
%	1	1	--	1	1
Other	476	1329	673	998	3476
%	7	11	15	28	13
TOTAL	2603	3302	1451	1795	9151
%	38	27	32	50	34
Other Borrowers	355	247	605	289	1496
%	5	2	13	8	5
TOTAL[1]	6858	12370	4491	3566	27285

Source: IMF Survey, February 1975

1. Totals differ from those reported in table 9 because of variations in reporting coverage.

Table 12

EXTERNAL DOLLAR POSITIONS OF REPORTING EUROPEAN BANKS
December 1973 - December 1974

($ billions)

	Dec 1973	June 1974	Dec 1974
	LIABILITIES TO		
Inside Area	69.9	70.4	69.1
Other Europe	11.6	13.7	14.4
Canada	5.7	5.0	4.5
Caribbean Area	6.1	8.7	8.5
Singapore	0.7	1.2	1.0
Middle East	6.2	15.4	24.0
US	10.1	12.0	12.6
Japan	3.4	4.2	3.5
Other	14.9	18.2	17.8
Unallocated	2.8	2.9	0.3
TOTAL	131.4	151.7	155.7
	CLAIMS ON		
Inside Area	64.2	64.7	61.1
Other Europe	12.0	14.9	16.3
Canada	3.9	2.9	2.4
Caribbean Area	12.1	16.3	15.4
Singapore	1.7	2.2	3.0
Middle East	2.1	2.1	2.9
US	14.1	19.2	18.7
Japan	7.5	13.7	14.5
Other	14.1	17.7	20.7
Unallocated	0.4	0.5	0.7
TOTAL	132.1	154.2	155.7
	NET POSITIONS[1]		
Inside Area	- 5.7	- 5.7	- 8.0
Other Europe	0.4	1.2	1.9
Canada	- 1.8	- 2.1	- 2.1
Caribbean Area	6.0	7.6	6.9
Singapore	1.0	1.0	2.0
Middle East	- 4.1	-13.3	-21.1
US	4.0	7.2	6.1
Japan	4.1	9.5	11.0
Other	- 0.8	- 0.5	2.9
Unallocated	- 2.4	- 2.4	0.4
TOTAL	0.7	2.5	--

Source: BIS Annual Report, 1975

1. Negative sign denotes net liabilities.

Table 13
ESTIMATED DEPLOYMENT OF OIL-EXPORTING COUNTRIES' SURPLUSES[1]
1974

($ billions and %)

	Q_1		Q_2		Q_3		Q_4	
eign currency deposits in London	2.5		4.5		3.4		3.4	
%	36		29		21		20	
eign currency deposits elsewhere	1.5		3.5		1.5		2.5	
%	21		23		9		14	
tal foreign currency deposits		4.0		8.0		4.9		[illegible]
%		57		52		30		[illegible]
llar deposits in US	0.6		0.8		2.3		0.3	
%	9		5		14		2	
erling deposits in UK	-0.1		0.7		1.1		---	
%	(1)		5		7		---	
tal US/UK deposits		0.5		1.5		3.4		[illegible]
%		7		10		21		
BANK DEPOSITS		4.5		9.5		8.3		[illegible]
%		64		61		51		[illegible]
ERNMENT SECURITIES		0.5		1.4		2.3		[illegible]
%		7		9		14		[illegible]
ERNMENT SECURITIES		0.8		0.8		0.9		[illegible]
%		11		5		6		

NCY LENDING TO UK	---	0.5	0.3	0.4
%	---	3	2	2
ORGANISATIONS	---	0.5	0.8	2.3
%	---	3	5	13
	1.2	2.8	3.7	5.6
%	17	18	23	32
ENT OF SURPLUSES	7.0	15.5	16.3	17.4

of England Quarterly Bulletin, June 1975

Bahrein, Brunei, Ecuador, Gabon, Indonesia, Iran, Iraq, Kuwait, Libya, Nigeria, Oman, Qatar, Saudi Arabia, T nited Arab Emirates and Venezuela.

(i) equities and property, (ii) special bilateral facilities, (iii) loans to less-developed countries.

Table 14

COMPOSITION AND DISTRIBUTION OF INTERNATIONAL RESERVES 1973 - 1974

($ billions and %)

	1973	1974	Change	% Change
RESERVE COMPOSITION				
Gold	43.2	43.7	0.5	1
SDRs	10.6	10.9	0.3	3
Reserve positions in IMF	7.5	10.9	3.4	45
Non-dollar exchange reserves	18.5	24.3	5.8	31
Dollar claims on US	66.8	76.5	9.7	15
Identified holdings of Euro-dollars	25.1	40.0	14.9	59
of which: Major oil-exporting countries	4.9	19.8	14.9	304
Industrial countries	8.8	7.8	(1.0)	(11)
Other countries	11.4	12.4	1.0	9
Residual	11.0	12.0	1.0	9
TOTAL RESERVES	182.6	218.2	35.6	19
RESERVE DISTRIBUTION				
Industrial countries	115.8	120.1	4.3	4
of which: US	14.4	16.0	1.6	11
UK	6.5	7.0	0.5	8
Germany	33.2	32.4	(0.8)	(2)
Japan	12.3	13.5	1.2	10
Other	49.4	51.2	1.8	4
Primary producing countries (more-developed)	24.2	21.3	(2.9)	(12)
Primary producing countries (less-developed) (excluding major oil-exporting countries)	28.1	30.1	2.0	7
Major oil-exporting countries	14.5	46.6	32.1	221
TOTAL RESERVES	182.6	218.2	35.6	19

Source: IMF Annual Report, 1975

Table 15

ERNAL POSITIONS OF REPORTING EUROPEAN BANKS IN DOLLARS AND OTHER CURRENC
1963 - 1974

($ millions and %)

	1963[2]	1964	1965	1966	1967	1968	1969	1970	1971[3]	1972	19
E S											
	7390	9650	11390	14770	18120	26870	46200	58700	70750	96730	130
	74	79	80	80	81	80	81	78	72	73	6
	2630	2570	2820	3700	4330	6890	10640	16590	26980	35200	60
	10020	12220	14210	18470	22450	33760	56840	75290	97730	131930	191
	7670	9000	11590	16070	19890	30430	47630	60370	71500	98000	133
	73	75	77	79	80	80	82	77	71	74	7
	2820	3030	3550	4180	4960	7400	10700	17880	28630	33840	54
	10490	12030	15140	20250	24850	37830	58330	78250	100130	131840	188

nnual Report, various issues

Marks, Swiss francs, sterling, French francs, guilders and lire.
r 1963 is end of third quarter, all others are end of year.
series -- figures exclude Swiss trustee funds.
xclude currency positions of the BIS, but include certain long-term positions previously excluded.

Table 16

EURO-CURRENCY POSITIONS OF UK BANKS
1968 - 1974

($ billions)

	Apr 1968	Jul 1969	Jul 1970	Feb 1971	Oct 1971	Oct 1972	Mar 1973	Sep 1973	Mar 1974	May 1974
TIES										
Banks[1]	6.1	11.8	16.5	16.9	18.5	25.7	31.0	36.9	41.8	43.8
s	8.4	21.3	23.4	24.9	28.9	34.2	43.7	47.2	58.2	62.7
ium Banks					3.1	6.5	8.4	9.5	12.0	12.4
e Banks	2.9	4.9	6.6	9.4	8.7	12.9	7.3	10.1	17.0	19.5
anks							10.1	16.0	19.9	19.4
	17.3	38.1	46.6	51.3	59.1	79.2	100.6	119.9	148.9	157.8
Banks[1]	6.2	11.9	16.6	17.0	18.6	25.8	31.2	37.1	41.9	43.8
s	8.4	21.3	23.3	24.8	28.9	34.1	43.7	47.1	58.2	62.5
ium Banks					3.2	6.6	8.6	9.8	12.1	12.5
e Banks	2.8	4.9	6.6	9.4	8.7	12.9	7.3	10.1	17.0	19.5
anks							10.1	16.0	19.9	19.4
	17.3	38.1	46.5	51.3	59.4	79.3	100.8	120.1	149.1	157.7

Bank of England Quarterly Bulletin, various issues

ludes Commonwealth banks.

SELECTED BIBLIOGRAPHY

ALLEN, R. "Can the Eurocurrency Market Finance the Oil Deficits?", The Banker November 1974, pp. 1295-1341.

ALTMAN, O.L. "Foreign Markets for Dollars, Sterling and Other Currencies", IMF Staff Papers (Vol. VIII) 1961, pp. 313-354.

--- "Canadian Markets for US Dollars", IMF Staff Papers (Vol IX) 1962, pp. 297-313.

--- "Recent Developments in Foreign Markets for Dollars and Other Currencies", IMF Staff Papers (Vol X) 1963, pp. 48-93.

--- "Euro-dollars: Some Further Comments", IMF Staff Papers (Vol. XII) 1965, pp. 1-14.

ARGY, V. & HODJERA, Z. "Financial Integration and Interest Rate Linkages in the Industrial Countries", IMF Staff Papers (Vol. XX) 1973, pp. 1-77.

ASHBY, D. "Analysing the Maturity Structure of the Euro-dollar Market", The Banker July 1973, pp. 769-772.

--- "The $300 billion Super-dollar Market", The Banker May 1974, pp. 449-454.

ATKIN, J. "Eurodollar Interest Rates", The Banker January 1973, pp. 25-28.

BANK OF ENGLAND QUARTERLY BULLETIN. Various issues, including:

--- "UK Banks' External Liabilities and

Claims in Foreign Currencies", June 1964, pp. 100-108.

--- "The London Dollar Certificate of Deposit", December 1973, pp. 446-452.

--- "The Euro-currency Business of Banks in London", March 1970, December 1970, June 1971, March 1972, March 1973, September 1973, March 1974, September 1974.

BANK FOR INTERNATIONAL SETTLEMENTS ANNUAL REPORT. Various issues.

BANKER, THE. "The Euro-dollar Market -- What it means for London", August 1969, pp. 773-781.

--- "Ebb Tide for Euro-dollars?", March 1973, pp. 251-254.

--- "US Capital Markets Re-open", September 1975, pp. 1053-1054.

BELL, G.L. "Credit Creation Through Euro-dollars", The Banker August 1964, pp. 494-502.

--- The Eurodollar Market and the International Financial System, Macmillan, London 1973.

BLACK, S.W. "An Econometric Study of Euro-dollar Borrowing by New York Banks and the Rate of Interest on Euro-dollars", Journal of Finance March 1971, pp. 83-88.

BLONDEEL, J.L. "A Decade of Eurobond Financing", The Banker June 1974, pp. 561-562.

--- "Outlook for Eurocredits", The Banker July 1974, pp. 761-762.

BRANDTS. "An Introduction to Lending in the Euro-currency Market", August 1973.

BRANSON, W. & HILL, P. "Capital Movements in the O.E.C.D. Area", OECD Economic Outlook December 1971, pp. 42-52.

BRIMMER, A. "The Federal Reserve Looks at the Role of Euro-dollars", The Banker April 1969, pp. 352-355.

BROWN, B. Money, Hard and Soft, Macmillan, London 1978.

BRUNSDEN, P.J. "The US Prime Rate", The Banker July 1973, pp. 773-778.

--- "The Money Markets: A Guide", *The Banker* September 1973, pp. 1031-1039.

CAIRNCROSS, A. *Control of Long-term International Capital Movements*, The Brookings Institution, Washington D.C. 1973.

CAMPBELL, M. "Term Structure of the Eurocurrency Markets", *The Banker* April 1973, pp. 372-376.

CARLI, G. "Eurodollars: A Paper Pyramid", *Banca Nazionale del Lavoro Quarterly Review* June 1971, pp. 95-109.

CHALMERS, E. *Readings in the Euro-dollar*, W.P. Griffith and Sons, London 1969.

--- "International Interest Rate War", *The Banker* July 1970, pp. 706-716.

CHRISTIE, H. "Euro-dollars and the Balance of Payments", *The Banker* May 1967, pp. 34-45.

CLENDENNING, E.W. "Euro-dollars: The Problem of Control", *The Banker* April 1968, pp. 321-329.

--- *The Euro-dollar Market*, Clarendon Press, Oxford 1970.

--- "Euro-dollars and Credit Creation", *International Currency Review* March/April 1971, pp. 12-19.

COOMBS, C.A. *The Arena of International Finance*, John Wiley and Sons, New York 1976.

COOPER, R.N. "The Interest Equalization Tax: An Experiment in the Separation of Capital Markets", *Finanzarchiv* December 1965, pp. 447-471.

--- "Eurodollars, Reserve Dollars, and Asymmetries in the International Monetary System", *Journal of International Economics* September 1972, pp. 325-344.

DAVIS, S.I. "A Buyers' Market in Euro-dollars", *Harvard Business Review* May/June 1973, pp. 119-130.

DEUTSCHE BUNDESBANK. *Monthly Report of the Deutsche Bundesbank*. Various issues.

--- Report of the Deutsche Bundesbank (Annual). Various issues.

DUFFEY, G. & GIDDY, I. The International Money Market, Prentice-Hall, New Jersey 1978.

EINZIG, P. The Euro-bond Market (2nd ed.), Macmillan, London 1969.

--- The Euro-dollar System (5th ed.), Macmillan, London 1973.

--- Roll-over Credits, Macmillan, London 1973.

--- & QUINN, B.S. The Euro-dollar System (6th ed.), Macmillan, London 1977.

EURO-MARKET LETTER. Published by The Financial Times. Various issues.

EURO-MONEY. Various issues.

EVITT, H. A Manual of Foreign Exchange (7th ed.) revised by R.F. Pither, Pitman, London 1971.

FEDERAL RESERVE BANK OF CHICAGO. Euro-dollars -- A Selected Bibliography (3rd ed.) September 1970, and Supplement November 1971.

FEDERAL RESERVE BANK OF CLEVELAND: ECONOMIC REVIEW. "The Euro-dollar Market: The Anatomy of a Deposit and Loan Market", Pt.I - March 1970, pp. 3-19; Pt. II - April 1970, pp. 3-17; Pt. III - May 1970, pp. 3-14.

FEDERAL RESERVE BULLETIN. Various issues, including:

--- "Euro-dollars: A Changing Market", October 1969, pp. 765-783.

FINANCIAL STATISTICS. CSO London. Various issues.

FINANCIAL TIMES. Various issues.

FIRST NATIONAL CITY BANK (now CITIBANK) MONTHLY ECONOMIC LETTER. "Euromoney and Inflation -- Guilt by Association?", February 1976, pp. 9-12.

FRATIANNI, M. & SAVONA, P. "Eurodollar Creation: Comments on Prof. Machlup's Propositions and Developments", Banca Nazionale del

Lavoro Quarterly Review June 1971, pp. 110-125.

FRIEDMAN. M. "The Euro-dollar Market: Some First Principles", Morgan Guaranty Survey October 1969 (offprint).

GRAUWE, P. de. "The Development of the Euro-currency Market", Finance and Development September 1975, pp. 14-16.

HARROD, R. Money, Macmillan, London 1969.

HEWSON, J. Liquidity Creation and Distribution in the Eurocurrency Markets, Lexington Books, US 1975.

--- & SAKAKIBARA, E. "The Euro-dollar Deposit Multiplier -- A Portfolio Approach", IMF Staff Papers (Vol. XXI) 1974, pp. 307-328.

--- The Eurocurrency Markets and Their Implications, Lexington Books, US 1975.

HINSHAW, R. (ed.) Inflation as a Global Problem, John Hopkins University Press, Baltimore and London 1972.

HOLMES, A.R. & KLOPSTOCK, F.H. "The Market for Dollar Deposits in Europe", Federal Reserve Bank of New York Monthly Review November 1960, pp. 197-202.

INTERNATIONAL MONETARY FUND. Annual Report. Various issues.

--- International Financial Statistics. Various issues.

--- Monthly Survey. Various issues.

KERN, D. "International Finance and the Euro-dollar Market", National Westminster Bank Review November 1971, pp. 6-21.

KINDLEBERGER, C.P. "The Euro-dollar and the Internationalization of US Monetary Policy", Banca Nazionale del Lavoro Quarterly Review March 1969, pp. 3-15.

KLOPSTOCK, F.H. "The International Money Market: Structure, Scope and Instruments", Journal of Finance May 1965, pp. 182-208.

--- The Euro-dollar Market: Some Unresolved Issues, Essays in International Finance no.65, Princeton University March 1968.

--- "Euro-dollars in the Liquidity and Reserve Management of United States Banks", Federal Reserve Bank of New York Essays in Domestic and International Finance, August 1969, pp. 72-80.

--- "Money Creation in the Euro-dollar Market -- A Note on Professor Friedman's Views", Federal Reserve Bank of New York Monthly Review January 1970, pp. 12-15.

--- "The Wiring of the Euro-dollar Market", Euromoney August 1970, pp. 16-20.

KVASNICKA, J.C. "Euro-dollars -- An Important Source of Funds for American Banks", Federal Reserve Bank of Chicago: Business Conditions June 1969, pp. 9-20.

LAMFALUSSY, A. "The Eurobond Market", Journal of the Institute of Bankers April 1968, pp. 142-155.

LEE, B.E. The Euro-dollar Market (unpublished Ph.D. thesis, Manchester 1972).

--- "The Euro-dollar Multiplier", Journal of Finance September 1973, pp. 867-874.

LITTLE, J.S. "The Euro-dollar Market: Its Nature and Impact", Federal Reserve Bank of Boston: New England Economic Review May/June 1969, pp. 2-31.

--- Euro -dollars: The Money Market Gypsies, Harper and Row, New York 1975.

LLEWELLYN, D.T. "How to Control Capital Flows", The Banker July 1973, pp. 764-768.

--- International Financial Integration, Macmillan, London 1980.

LOW, W.F. "What Medium Term Financing is all about", The Banker July 1972, pp. 929-931.

LUTZ, F.A. "The Euro-currency System", Banca Nazionale del Lavoro Quarterly Review September 1974, pp. 183-200.

McCLAM, W. "Credit Substitution and the Euro-currency Market", Banca Nazionale del Lavoro Quarterly Review September 1972, pp. 324-363.

McKENZIE, G.W. The Economics of the Euro-Currency System, Macmillan, London 1976.

McKINNON, R.I. The Euro Currency Market, Essays in International Finance no.125, Princeton University December 1977.

McMAHON, C.W. "Controlling the Euromarkets", Paper delivered at a Financial Times conference, February 5th 1976. (Reprinted in Bank of England Quarterly Bulletin March 1976, pp. 74-77).

McRAE, H. "So what happens when the IET comes off?", Euromoney January 1974, pp. 41-43.

MACHLUP, F. "Euro-dollar Creation: A Mystery Story", Banca Nazionale del Lavoro Quarterly Review September 1970, pp. 220-260.

--- "The Magicians and their Rabbits", Morgan Guaranty Survey May 1971, pp. 3-13.

--- "Euro-dollars, Once Again", Banca Nazionale del Lavoro Quarterly Review June 1972, pp. 119-137.

--- "Five Errors about the Eurodollar System", Euromoney July 1972, pp. 8-14.

MAKIN, J.H. "Demand and Supply Functions for Stocks of Euro-dollar Deposits: An Empirical Study", The Review of Economics and Statistics November 1972, pp. 381-391.

--- "Identifying a Reserve Base for the Euro-dollar System", Journal of Finance June 1973, pp. 609-617.

MARCUS, E. & MARCUS, M.R. "Euro-dollars and the Money Supply", The Banker April 1970, pp. 398-403.

MARSTON, R.C. American Monetary Policy and the Structure of the Eurodollar Market, Princeton Studies in International Finance no.34, Princeton University 1974.

MAYER, H.W. Some Theoretical Problems Relating to the Euro-dollar Market, Essays in International Finance no.79, Princeton

University 1970.

--- "Multiplier Effects and Credit Creation in the Euro-dollar Market", Banca Nazionale del Lavoro Quarterly Review September 1971, pp. 233-262.

--- "Some Analytical Aspects of the Intermediation of Oil Surpluses by the Euro-currency Market", Banca Nazionale del Lavoro Quarterly Review September 1974, pp. 201-226.

--- "The BIS Concept of the Eurocurrency Market", Euromoney May 1976, pp. 60-66.

MENDELSOHN, M.S. "The Eurobond and Capital Market Integration", Journal of Finance March 1972, pp. 110-126.

--- "The Euromarkets in the World Economy", The Banker January 1976, pp. 49-65.

MIKESELL, R.F. "The Euro-dollar Market and the US International Accounts", Euromoney January 1970, pp. 44-45.

--- "Foreign Dollar Balances in the United States", Euromoney February 1972, pp. 14-19.

--- "The Euro-dollar Market and the Foreign Demand for Liquid Dollar Assets", Journal of Money, Credit and Banking August 1972, pp. 643-683.

--- & FURTH, J. H. Foreign Dollar Balances and the International Role of the Dollar, Studies in International Economic Relations no.8, National Bureau of Economic Research, New York 1974.

MOHAMMAD, A.F. & SACCOMANNI, F. "Short-term Banking and Euro-currency Credits to Developing Countries", IMF Staff Papers (Vol. XX) 1973, pp. 612-638.

MORGAN GUARANTY TRUST COMPANY. "The Financing of Business with Euro-dollars", (offprint) New York 1969.

NIEHANS, J. & HEWSON, J. "The Eurodollar Market and Monetary Theory", Journal of Money, Credit and Banking (Vol. VIII, 1) 1976, pp. 1-27.

OSSOLA, R. "Central Bank Interventions and Eurocurrency Markets", Banca Nazionale del Lavoro Quarterly Review March 1973, pp.29-45.

OWENS, J.P. Growth of the Euro-dollar Market, Bangor Occasional Papers in Economics no.4, University of Wales Press 1974.

PARK, Y.S. The Euro-bond Market, Praeger Special Studies in International Economics and Development, New York 1974.

PROCHNOW, H. (ed.) The Euro-dollar, Rand McNally, Chicago 1970.

QUINN, B.S. The New Euromarkets, Macmillan, London 1975.

RADICE, J. "The Eurobond Market Now", The Banker July 1972, pp. 925-928.

RUEFF, J. "How the Euromarkets Contribute to World Inflation", Euromoney April 1975, pp.16-18.

SAKAKIBARA, E. "The Euro-currency Market in Perspective", Finance and Development September 1975, pp.10-13.

SCOTT, I.O. Jr. "That Controversial Euro-dollar Market", National Westminster Bank Review August 1969, pp. 2-22.

SURVEY OF CURRENT BUSINESS. (US Department of Commerce). Various issues.

SWOBODA, A.K. The Euro-dollar Market: An Interpretation, Essays in International Finance no.64, Princeton University 1968.

TREASURY BULLETIN. (US Treasury Department). Various issues.

VAN DER MENSBRUGGHE, J.D.M. "Foreign Issues in Europe", IMF Staff Papers (Vol. XI) 1964, pp.327-335.

VON CLEMM, M. "The Rise of Consortium Banking", Harvard Business Review May/June 1971, pp. 125-142.

WALTERS, A.A. "The Longer Term Future for the Euromarkets", United Malayan Banking Corporation Economic Review (Vol. IX, 2) 1973, pp. 75-80.

WEISSMULLER, A.A. "London Consortium Banks", Journal of Institute of Bankers August 1974, pp. 203-217.

--- "Trends in Medium-term Lending", The Banker March 1976, pp. 261-267.

WORLD FINANCIAL MARKETS. (Morgan Guaranty Trust Company of New York). Various issues.

YASSUKOVICH, S. "Dilemmas in Euromarket Regulation", The Banker April 1973, pp. 368-371.

ZOMBANAKIS, M. "The Euro-dollar Market in Decline?", The Banker April 1972, pp. 547-548.

--- "Arab Funds and the Markets", The Banker July 1974, pp. 751-752.

INDEX

For Product Safety Concerns and Information please contact our
EU representative GPSR@taylorandfrancis.com Taylor & Francis
Verlag GmbH, Kaufingerstraße 24, 80331 München, Germany